Motherhood and Family

MOTHERHOOD AND FAMILY

RECLAIMING THE HEART OF THE HOME. FAITH, FEMININITY, AND CATHOLIC MOTHERHOOD

The *INTEGRITY* Series

Angelus Press

PO Box 217 | Saint Marys, KS 66536

Library of Congress Cataloging-in-Publication Data

Motherhood and family.
   p. cm. -- (From Integrity ; v. 4)
   ISBN 978-1-892331-63-2
   1.   Motherhood--Religious aspects--Catholic Church. 2.   Marriage--Religious aspects--Catholic Church. 3.   Mothers--Religious life. 4.   Wives--Religious life. 5.   Catholic women--Religious life.
   BX2353.M68 2008
   248.8'431088282--dc22

                                                            2008049684

ANGELUS PRESS
PO BOX 217
SAINT MARYS, KANSAS 66536
PHONE (816) 753-3150
FAX (816) 753-3557
ORDER LINE 1-800-966-7337
www.angeluspress.org

ISBN 978-1-892331-63-2
FIRST PRINTING—January 2009
SECOND EDITION—September 2020
SECOND EDITION, SECOND PRINTING—October 2021

Printed in the United States of America

CONTENTS

FOREWORD. VII

CHILDREN AND
CREATIVE ACTIVITY *Caryll Houselander*. I
(August 1952, Vol. 6, No. 11, pp. 8-19)

CHILDREN AND THE
IMITATION OF MARY *Mary Reed Newland* 15
(May 1952, Vol. 6, No. 8, pp. 34-39)

THE LOVE-EDUCATION
OF GIRLS *Marion Mitchell Stancioff* 23
(August 1949, Vol. 3, No. 11, pp. 26-34)

TEACHING CHILDREN
TO PRAY *Mary Reed Newland*. 37
(August 1949, Vol. 3, No. 11, pp. 18-23)

MOTHERS OF SAINTS *Sister Mariel, S.S.S.*. 47
(April 1951, Vol. 5, No. 7, pp. 21-29)

RECREATION AND CHILDREN *Mary Reed Newland* . . . 57
(July 1953, Vol. 7, No. 10, pp. 25-32)

ON HAVING BABIES AT HOME 69
(February, 1950, Vol. 4, No. 5, pp. 29-42)

BREASTFEEDING *Mary Reed Newland* 89
(August 1953, Vol. 7, No. 11, pp. 31-37)

MARRIAGE AND
SPIRITUALITY *Mary Reed Newland*. 99
(October 1951, Vol. 6, No. 11, pp. 24-33)

"HE MARRIED AN ANGEL" *Susan Candle*. 115
(December 1953, Vol. 8, No. 3, pp. 2-13)

POVERTY AND MARRIAGE *Ed Willock* 133
(May 1949, Vol. 3, No. 8, pp. 32-37)

ONE AND ONE IS ONE *Ed Willock* 143

MOTHERS-IN-LAW *Mary Reed Newland* 155
(March 1951, Vol. 5, No. 6, pp. 11-17)

THE SPIRITUALITY
OF MARRIED LIFE *Elizabeth M. Sheehan* 165
(November 1948, Vol. 3, No. 2, pp. 26-35)

THE TRAGEDY OF
MODERN WOMAN *Carol Jackson* 179
(November 1948, Vol. 3, No. 2, pp. 3-10)

THE LATTER DAY *Elaine Malley* 191
(September 1953, Vol. 7, No. 12, pp. 29-35)

FOREWORD

Integrity was a Catholic magazine that died during the 50s along with the rest of Catholic literature. Both were the natural product of a society which possessed a living Catholic Faith. Published from 1946-1955, *Integrity* focused on family issues and intellectual questions with an impact on daily Catholic life. The present volume is a selection of essays on the role of the Christian woman, entitled *Motherhood and Family*.

Although written prior to the revolution of '68, the questions raised in this book are essentially a defense of the Christian concept of social life and institutions against a revolutionary concept which reproaches the Christian woman to be only about "church, children and kitchen." This book definitely does not follow this latter type of paradigm, but rather applies the eternally true principles of Christian doctrine to the encounters of Christian women and "modern" society. You will find, for example, a reflection about marriage starting with the anecdote of a young single woman who was, in order to be convinced of the benefits of married life, confronted with the "perfect couple." She met them and was impressed. Some months later she was called by the man who asked her if she could help to "talk to the light of his life"? He had incurred serious losses in his finances–"and suddenly, life was real, life was earnest. He was able to bear up under it, but apparently she wasn't..."

Subsequently the woman opened her heart about the challenges she is meeting: "My dear, you can't know what a mess it all is. I hate working, but I have to or we can't live the way we do, and Jack simply doesn't understand what its doing to me."

So far you follow the story, thinking that these people were not prepared for marriage, having no idea of the spirit of sacrifice that it requires. But the woman continues:

"Then to complicate things even more, his mother's been here for two weeks and I had to move all my clothes out and take a temporary apartment downstairs."

"Why the apartment downstairs? Don't tell me you can't put up with your mother-in-law for just two weeks?"

"My mother-in-law?" and the other woman screamed. "Oh darling! You don't understand–we aren't even married!"

Sudden turns sometimes give an opening to new perspectives. Not married? So what about the "perfect couple" if you take a look behind the facade? Not much, apparently, without money and–God…

These are the type of reflections we are confronted with in this book: Catholic, dedicated, convinced, modern (in the good sense). It is exactly what we need in order to regain confidence in the institutions of the Church, its teaching and in women and the possibilities of human nature.

Blessed Virgin Mary, cause of our joy, pray for us.

Fr. Markus Heggenberger
November 5, 2008

CHILDREN AND CREATIVE ACTIVITY

Caryll Houselander

Art is not just for the talented child. For children, and grown-ups, too, working with their hands and making things actually helps teach the love of God the Creator and of our neighbor, too.

If you study a diagram of the human brain you will see that almost a third of it is designed to control the movements of the hands. This ceases to surprise when you consider all that a man can do with his hands, and how different the things he does will be, according to what is in his mind.

One man will inflict a wound, another will heal one with his hands; one will strike, another will caress. There is an almost inexhaustible list of these things men do or can do with their hands, from the laying on of hands by the Bishop in Confirmation to the mother's hand holding the tiny one of her small child to reassure it in the dark.

The thing I want to consider now is *making things* with the hands, especially the things that artists make, and above all what we learn from watching children making things. I say what *we* learn, because I am certain that we cannot teach children "art," but we can learn many deep, often buried, and essential things about human nature itself, and about

1

individual children and their needs, by watching them discover its meaning for themselves. It was through chance more than anything else that a group of oddly assorted children became, literally for me, the fortunes of war, and quite by chance that I discovered from them the power to heal and integrate that lies in art or, if you like, just in making things.

These children were refugees from Europe, very literally orphans from the storm of war, who in most cases had lost everything and I mean everything, not only their homes and their country, but their sense of security, their trust in mankind, and sometimes their own integrity. Many of them were suffering from shock, and their recent experiences had, I imagined, brought to the surface symptoms of difficulties that were there before, perhaps inherent, but had been unsuspected.

They came from every strata of society, from professions and trades and business; some were the children of scavengers, some were intellectual types, others natural manual laborers. Their ages ranged from four years old to eighteen, but they brought younger ones to my one-room "school," and on one occasion, a father with a fierce black moustache and the manner of a brigand—who presented himself as "a pupil" with such insistence that it finally became necessary to form a small class of adults too.

I was supposed to teach these children, though less from the point of view of educating them than of occupying them, in order—since none of them fitted into the real schools—to keep them from running wild in the streets, on which German bombs happened to be falling with depressing regularity day and night. With the passing of the years since then, I have made friends with many other children who in one way or another were adrift, some from behind the Iron Curtain, some from close at home, but who were "retarded" or "delinquent" or in some other way "maladjusted." But what I could do for these others was given to me and taught to me by that first motley crowd of refugees.

COMMUNICATION

Our first difficulty was how to speak to each other. They did not speak my language, I did not speak theirs, they did not all speak each other's—we were in a tower of Babel! There was only one way out, to do, as the cave men did, say what we wanted to by drawing pictures. After all, handwriting is only drawing countless tiny pictures of what is in your mind, and it started by the pictures the cave man drew on the walls of his cave.

Those pictures in the caves were not only messages about danger and hunger and such things; they were also, and perhaps oftener, pictures which said that the man who had made them rejoiced in the sheer vitality and beauty of the thing he drew, that in his heart there was delight in something, some animal or bird, or the shining of the sun, or an occupation of his own, like hunting, or making tools and weapons; and he could not contain this delight, he must share it with others, and the only way he could do that was to throw it outside himself, out of the wordless inward abstraction of his secret, inarticulate mind into concrete, visible form. Thus and only thus could he give shape and color to his inward joy, and so give his joy to other men.

In the earliest cave drawings we do not see merely a drawing of an animal, but of what a certain man delighted in about a particular animal. There is nothing photogenic in these drawings; they are quite selective. Some show just the two or three long swinging lines that point to the rhythm rippling through the body of that wild beast, others the streak of his swift flight, just that which the artist loved, and nothing else, nothing superfluous, nothing unnecessary.

THE VAGUE AND TTERRIBLE FEARS

As I have said, the earliest drawings were sometimes pictures not of what a man delighted in but of what he feared. They might be something he feared in his own secret soul, and which was all the more frightening because it was formless. He must, if he was to overcome it, come face to face with it and look it squarely in the eyes. This could only be done, in the case of a real "bogey" (an abstract thing in his own inner consciousness), by giving it shape and form himself, so that he could look at it and, still more important, put it under his own control.

As men developed there arose a superstition among some of them that if a person allowed himself to be drawn he fell into the power of the artist. To this day gypsies will refuse to be drawn or photographed, because they believe that he who has their image has power over them. Children are in a sense primitive people. Every little child is a cave man, a new man in a world which to him is new.

Nearly every child is inarticulate about that which concerns him most deeply. When he reaches an age in which he has emotional responses to other people he is almost totally unable to express them, especially in words. About that which causes him to suffer, and about the vague yet terrible fears which invade him in secret, he is usually dumb.

With a young child then, art (in this case I mean drawing pictures, or making things in putty or some such substance) is as truly as it was to primitive men, a means of *communication* and of *liberation*. This I discovered very early among my refugee children: give them paper and paint and crayons and putty, and they will be able, even if you cannot (as I could not) speak their language, to tell you what is within them.

Now it is a necessity to all human beings to reveal the secrets of their soul—to express their inmost love, their secret joy, to externalize their hidden, and often unformulated fears. To do that is the simplest and most primitive use of art. There was one little boy who had a bogey of his own, some buried terror which, though (and largely because) he could not describe it to anyone, had made of him a mass of nerves, a victim of habits that exasperated his family, and not only anti-social to other children, but, if they ever made advances to him, positively aggressive in his self-defense. Inevitably their "advances" changed to teasing and unconscious cruelty.

This little boy began to make things with putty. At first he made potatoes and rather shapeless little animals. He never looked up while he worked. He never—if he could help it—allowed anyone to see what he made. If anyone approached him while he was at work he tried to cover his little table with his body. Then one day he made his bogey. This time he did not hide it, but led me by the hand to it. There could be no possible doubt that it was meant to be a horrible thing, and certainly he had achieved that—the tiny image looked almost obscene.

The little boy looked at it with an expression of triumph. There was his bogey, that formless, colorless, nebulous horror that no one had been able to kill because no one could see it or touch it, given shape and substance, and made small enough to be crushed in *his* hand.

He had made it, it was smaller than he, it was within his power, and he could kill it!

Kill it he did, crushing it back into shapelessness and then breaking it into pieces.

It was after that that he began to play with other children.

ART IS COMMUNION

When the artist, child or man, makes an image, not of what he fears, but of what he loves—his art is more than communication, it is *communion* with others. It is the means by which he gives the wonder of his inward self to other people, and when they respond to him by delighting in the thing he has made, it is because it also expresses that which was inarticulate in their own souls. In the thing of beauty made by a man's hands, the thing into which he has put his own life, other men recognize the secrets of their own inward lives. This is why we love old tables and chairs and such things, polished by the touch of many caressing hands, and why we want to touch them with our own hands. It is our response to the craftsman who is long dead, but whose life still comes to us in his work, our communion with someone no longer on earth, through the thing he made on earth.

A little French girl among my children made birds from scraps of felt and organdy, which were so exquisite that everyone who looked at them laughed with joy. They showed the winged, dancing quality of the child's inward life, and though they were only little pieces of material, somehow they spoke of freedom, of rising into the pure blue summer skies as effortlessly as the lark. With a trueness of instinct that was characteristic of her, this little girl brought her bright birds to the grey basement used for an airraid shelter. It was her communion with us all, who longed for freedom and skies into which our hearts could ascend again.

ONE'S OWN MEDIUM

I have mentioned various materials. It is important for children—for everyone—to choose their own materials. Those children in school who are restricted to one medium because it is more convenient for the teacher are to be pitied. They will miss one of the most essential things in art—that which I call its sacramental quality.

Children should be given every kind of material that they can be given. Mud, sand, wood, paints, felt, paper, metal, water, putty and so on. God, after all, has given every substance in the world to them; He has given them seed and earth and seas and stars, shells and flowers and leaves and grass and stones and trees.

When the craftsman lays his hands upon the material into which he can most easily pour his own secret life, his touch is a caress; it is the touch of love. He will know at once that this is the substance which can receive his dream, this it is that shaped by his hands will be the shape of his shapeless longing, and will contain that which is within him and yet his heart cannot contain.

A man is never really whole until he has found that material which is for him the potential substance of his dreams. For one it will be that (to me) most beautiful of all substances, wood—wood which *lives* under the carver's hand. Another will discover his medium in earth, the rich soil that he can dig and sow and tend, until it seems to him that the spring he longed for all winter flowers from his own finger tips. Others will, like my little French girl, find woollen and cotton materials, or silk. And there are other substances to which we shall refer later, dough and flour and all the things women use to cook with, which also, through the loving contact of human hands, give tangible form to the intangible secrets of the human soul.

A SACRAMENTAL LIFE

People who fail completely to make any contact through their hands with any substance that can take the shape of their thought, often become insane—or perhaps it is because they are already insane that they lack the capacity. The mind which is absolutely unable to tether its dreams to anything tangible, or to give them shape and solidity in any material, or to sow them in any solid earth, is likely to become more and more formless and to drift more and more uncontrollably into realms of unreality.

In this we have an example in a very wide sense of "Unless the seed falling into the earth die, it remaineth itself alone." Perhaps the supreme tragedy of being insane is that of being inescapably and always alone.

The reason why this contact with substance and this going out of himself into some visible substance, which he can see and touch, is so necessary to man, is because man is a sacramental creature and he is made in the likeness of God. The more closely his daily life expresses his likeness to God, the more sane, the more complete a man will be.

It is easy to see how the artist who puts his life into his clay or his wood is like God when we think of man's creation, of God taking the dust and breathing His life into it to make man. It becomes more and more obvious when we think how Christ, the Son of God, used the humblest substances as the medium through which to give His love to men; mud and spittle on the blind man's eyes, the medium of His mercy. Writing in the dust with His finger, the medium of compassion, and for the final miracle of love, the gift of *Himself,* the simplest of all substances, bread. As if to remind us day after day that our life is by God's plan, the life of body and soul together, our supernatural life is given to us by the Church and continually renewed in us, sacramentally, through the use of the simplest substances, water, oil, salt, bread and wine.

Above all, we can see how artistic creation, approached as it should be, in humility and love, is a likeness to God, through the Incarnation. The Word of God, the unutterable Word of the Father's love is uttered in Christ. The boundless is bound in swaddling bands, the Word is made flesh.

A Liberation

This mystery was shown to me by the experience of one boy. He was an adolescent, full of turmoil and bitterness.

Every circumstance in his life had combined to twist him. He was above all afflicted by a sense of injustice and felt himself, in sheer angry self-defense, the enemy of society. If ever I have seen a human creature scourged and wounded and mocked by suffering, it was he. If ever I have seen one thrown down and crushed by the weight of the Cross, it was he. If ever I have seen one stripped naked and exposed to the misunderstanding, mockery and reproach of the world, it was he.

The material he chose to work in was wood; and like the little boy with the bogey, he worked in a corner alone, hiding his efforts. But when the work was done, it was no bogey or imp, it was a crucifix, carved crudely, yet with amazing skill. And the face, *a face of terrible suffering, was smiling!* It was the face of the young carver himself, his own features unmistakably, but transformed by that amazing smile on the face of the Crucified Christ.

That boy changed. The sudden realization of himself *indwelt by Christ,* flooded the bitterness out of him, and he became "a Christ" to the others.

THE MEANING OF WORK

We have seen that art, making things, above all making one's own image and likeness, is a means of liberating and healing, and a means to communion. It teaches a child that basic lesson of life, the secrets of his own nature, that he is made in the likeness of God and in the pattern of Christ, and that in order to be happy through his humanity, he must live in the way that satisfies the needs, not of a cog in a machine, but of a man indwelt by God.

There is something else too, something immensely important that the child will learn from making things: the meaning of work, what work should be to a man or woman. There is a common delusion that work is a punishment for sin, a hideous necessity. That it is something to be endured for the money it brings in, but a person's real life only begins when he leaves his work and seeks distraction or amusement outside it. Yet for the average person, work takes up nearly the whole of his waking life! It is a mistake to suppose that work was intended, in the first place, to be a punishment for sin.

Work was not introduced into man's life *after* Adam sinned, but before, at the time when Adam's whole life was an uninterrupted awareness of God's presence, and his un-interrupted delight was a continual contemplation of God's goodness, beauty and love. Work was given to him as one means to that contemplation. While the first dew still shone on the grass, the waters still trembled in the breath of the Spirit, and man's soul was as pure as the water and the dew, "...the Lord God took the man, and put him into the garden of Eden to dress it and to keep it."

Man was to know God by reflecting God's joy in creating the world, in his own soul; his work was to be a way of entering into and sharing the experience of God Himself.

He was to know the marvel of seeing the seed that had fallen from his finger tips into the earth, flowering under his feet, and to know, in so far as a finite creature can know the Infinite, the God Who made the multitudinous beauty of the world, in stars, and moon and sun, and flowers, wind and water, shadows and light, and rejoiced because He had made it. "And God saw everything that he had made, and behold it was very good."

NO EASY CREATION

That which did follow on sin, as part of man's punishment was that his work was to become a painful effort to him. He was no longer able to make anything with the ease of a creator, no longer would beauty overflow from his heart spontaneously and pour from his hands, flooding the world with its life—no, now he must wrestle with nature, and the substances he would work in would not yield to him unless he literally strove with them in the sweat of his brow.

"In the sweat of thy face shalt thou eat bread, til thou return into the ground."

But Christ, Himself working in the sweat of His face, restored even this aspect of work to its glory, making it again a constant act of adoration. The artist, and I count a good craftsman as an artist, knows the cost of acquiring skill; it is only those who do approach their work with the artist's attitude who will go through the necessary years of daily effort, practice and patience. To become a skilled craftsman means imposing upon oneself the discipline that forms character.

It would be impossible, for example, for an impatient, careless man to become a skilled woodworker. The uninitiated watching a carpenter at work suppose it easy—and indeed nothing is more lovely than to watch the apparent ease with which he planes and cuts and fits his wood. The rhythmic, swinging movements of his arms, the long easy sweep of his plane, the shavings falling away lightly curled and thin as rose petals. And then the exactitude with which the pieces fit together and interlock, and all the time the man's obvious pride and pleasure in his work.

Yes, it looks easy, and it has become easy too for the master craftsman, but what long self-discipline has produced that ease in him, that precision and lightness of touch, that flowing movement, and what constant application has enabled him to sharpen and set his tools to cut clean and to know his different woods, with their special grains, and even their special moods! It is this apprenticeship that restores man's pride and dignity in work and fits him to do the work that makes his own soul luminous in the shadow of the Trinity.

Now if we turn back to the diagram of the brain and study it again, remembering the reasons why it is a need of man's nature to co-ordinate hands and mind, it no longer seems strange at all that so much of the brain has been made for that very purpose. But if we turn from this study to the study of our contemporary society, we cannot be surprised by the prevalent discontent, joylessness and lack of direction or purpose that is its depressing characteristic.

Co-ordinating Mind and Hands

How many people today ever use their hands intelligently? Indeed, how many there are who practically never use them at all! Above all, how many are there whose daily work means making something conceived in their own minds?

Again, how many are there who can *choose* the work they are to do all their lives? And among the few who can choose, how many are there in whom the artist has not been destroyed, so that ignorant of their real needs they are often rejecting their true happiness by their choice? Girls and boys go into factories at sixteen, or into shops or offices or one of the professions a year or two later. In the factories most people make, not a whole thing they want to, but part of something they probably never see whole.

Most people are working simply for the money they have to earn, and they only start to live when the day's work ends, and even then few start to live in any full sense, for most people go in search of machine-made entertainment and canned emotion. When I think of these sad multitudes, I am reminded of those children who are "backward" or "maladjusted," who so often have very poor co-ordination between their hands and their minds. The workers of the world today seem to me very like those children, they seem to have lost that co-ordination. I believe the only remedy for the tragedy of our industrial civilization is to restore it.

My theory is grounded in the belief that every human being is an artist, simply because he is made in God's image and indwelt by His spirit. The artist has been submerged in most men, but because it is his true nature, it can always be restored.

THE ARTIST IN THE CHILD

Again, I think of the backward children and of one in particular who, because she was regarded as "hopeless," typifies the sad multitude. This child lived in a slum. She came regularly to a little group of children to whom I gave materials to work in, and she watched them working. Because her hands were so clumsy she was a source of irritation to her own family and was shunned by other children. She dropped things, broke things, she ate dirtily, she could not tie bows or fasten buttons. She was retarded, and utterly incapable of speaking about what was in her mind. I need not add that she was a very discouraged child, already accepting herself as being useless, even despicable.

Yet she came to the group, fascinated by watching them, pathetically longing to do something like they did. She hovered on the outskirts, going round behind the chairs of the workers, staring. When the others had gone and I was mopping up the inevitable mess, this child stayed behind with me, usually watching with a faint pitiful smile.

One night she very gingerly took a rag and mopped up too. Then she did it night after night and came to do it well. From that time she began to have self-respect. Very slowly, very painfully she learned, by copying my hands, to tie bows, to fasten buttons, and crowning triumph, to brush and part her hair! And one day she sat down at the table with the others and began to make things with plasticene.

I have seen many other children learn this co-ordination of head and hands in just this slow painful way, and with just this growing self-respect and happiness. Craftsmen acquiring their skill. If *they* can restore the artist in themselves, so also can the adults of the world, but the adults, like the children, will only realize what it is that they lack and want if they *see* artists at work.

Artists are considered in these days to be something like freaks; "practical" people who do not realize that they are repressed artists themselves, mistrust them, and feel that they need some excuse, some justification for being artists. They are usually poor and, in the world's eyes, improvident, because for the sheer joy of their work they are content to remain poor.

CHILDREN AND THE IMITATION OF MARY

Mary Reed Newland

Were you told as a child that Our Lady weeps when a girl whistles? Or that Mary would never chew gum? Mary Reed Newland, herself the mother of five, writes this article to put an end to such ideas in the training of children.

There is probably no woman who ever lived more maligned at the hands of her admirers than the Mother of God. Out of the endless reservoir of her virtues, her wisdom, her beauty of body and soul, there has emerged a nightmarish parade of Marys, and more arty rubbish, trashy verse, and pure sugar has been spun in her praise than one has the heart or the head to calculate. That some of it is sincere and, in that light praiseworthy, need not be gone into here since the point of this piece is not to walk the tightrope between art and sincerity; but at least it can be said that even in the case of the praiseworthy frights created in her name, the effect can be, and often is, devastating. And as though it weren't bad enough to have so much trash about masquerading as tribute, the greatest devastation of all is the complete obliteration, for so many, of the real magnificence behind the saccharine curtain. The whole mess has a yeasty quality—left alone, in the warm temperature of a well-disposed imagination, it begins to work like a dough, growing and spreading until finally it fills the vessel and there is no room for more. And when it is the mind of a child that is filled, then the pity is double, because the transcending personality of the Mother of God, who should be the companion of their growing up, their model of virtue, their source of all grace, is reduced to nothing but confection treading pearly clouds and strangling in blue chiffon. She will serve them as a pretty distraction in their infancy, compel them to an outward display of Christian manners in their early school years, but when the chips are down and passion and temptation are to be faced at last, her substance is that of a creature in a pretty dream, the last woman under the sun to face, much less tackle, the problems that go hand in hand with human weakness.

Children need Mary

Children need Mary, from the very beginning. They need her when they are beginning to wake up to the world around them, to their place in it, to their bodies—so alive with interest and stimulation, pain and pleasure. And children want her. They want her because deep inside of every man is the desire to be loved and understood by someone whose devotion is unchanging and whose judgments are ever just. Human mothers are not paragons of virtue, unless and until, with grace, in that last final gasp they reach sanctity. And for all the tenacity of a small child's devotion to his mother, it is only a matter of time before he is forced to admit that mother is neither infallible nor impeccable. But Mary is.

The problem is not, primarily, to convince the Catholic parent that if we are to lead our children to Christ, we must lead them through Mary—that is pretty commonly understood. But the big struggle seems to lie in giving Mary to children in a form that is sustaining all through the years of their early childhood, up to and beyond adolescence, and into the years of a growing maturity—with the relationship between the child and Mary growing, not diminishing.

Perhaps the weak spot is this predilection for the Mary of the apparitions, to the neglect of the Mary of Nazareth. Not that the antidote for the distortion of Mary is a neglect of Our Lady of Lourdes, or Guadalupe, or La Salette, or Fatima, but the Mary of the apparitions totally divorced from her life on this earth is incomplete too, and not so much in danger of neglect as the former, but in danger of being transformed into something bordering on the superstitious. Or perhaps the trouble is the contrast between the abundant detail of the apparitions and the scarcity of it in her life in the Gospels. Her heroism is there, in the Gospels, but it is told with such understatement that it takes digging and thinking and meditating to find it, and we are too lazy to do that when we can pick up holy cards and take someone else's word for what she was like. But it is the Mary of the Gospels we must give our children to imitate, who once lived in the world they live in and who served God perfectly in it.

MARY'S LOVE FOR GOD

Mary served God perfectly because first of all she loved Him perfectly, and the first step in the imitation of Mary is to love God. It is no good to recommend Mary as, say, a model of humility if one does not know that it was out of love there grew humility. Without first love, and then the humility, the *Magnificat* is consummate pride.

Without the love, there would have been no heroic courage, and without the courage, no *Fiat*. Hers was an intimate knowledge of Scripture and the Prophets, and it was no mystery to Mary what end lay in store for the Messias. Perhaps the details were lacking, still hidden in the mind of God, but the end of it all had been familiar to her ever since she had learned to read. And yet at the age of fifteen, she had the courage to face the prospect of inevitable anguish and say, "Be it done unto me according to Thy word."

IMITATING HER PURITY

Then there is purity, another virtue children must be urged to imitate in Mary. Mary's was a rare and wonderful purity, and based—if we are to read the account of the Annunciation correctly—on a full knowledge of how the body functions. Gabriel told her she was to be the mother of a child—and she did not ponder it silently, but asked immediately: "How shall this be done, because I know not man?" I would be willing to wager that a picture of the fifteen-year-old Mary, dazzling as she was in her array of graces, virtues, talents, attributes, all the rest—but also with an orderly knowledge of sex and its functions, would leave many a pious Catholic in a state of deep shock. It shouldn't—there were no gaps in the glory she wove for God; it was a fabric made of her whole being, both her body and her soul, and in the perfect knowledge and ordering of the body's functions there is a giving of glory to God. More than anyone who ever lived, she gave Him glory—ignorance was not part of it. And yet we have vast numbers of parents who persist in the notion that Mary's chastity consists, in *toto*, of a kind of superficial modesty.

Imitation of Mary's chastity is premised first of all on knowing what chastity is, and if it is a denial, of what it is a denial. It seems to occur to very few that chastity is, in the first place, not a denial of anything—that it is a positive state, and not a negative. In the *second* place, it is a denial—but in the first, it is a giving. Chastity is not a sour apple. It is the full, ripe, beautiful fruit plucked and given to God. In the sense that, given to God, it cannot be consumed by one's self—then it is denial, but who defines the giving of gifts to a lover as denial? These things are the privileges that go with being in love, and Mary's chastity was, again, not a denial of her own full, capable, fertile humanity, but a giving of this to God because in her love she would hold back nothing.

NO SILLY STUFF

Obedience is another of her virtues that flows from her love of God. This is what parents overlook. This is the thing they so often miss when pressing the Mary-virtues on their young—both their *young* young and their older young. One is not virtuous for the sake of being virtuous, or else it is not virtue. One is virtuous for the love of God.

This is a revolutionary idea—at least when applied to the theory that the imitation of Our Lady begins and ends in acting like a lady. It is the enemy of all the sentimental nonsense which results in an over-elaborate piousness with pictures, holy cards, statues and the like. I shall never forget the account of a school piano recital given to me by a sweet, pious child of twelve.

"Oh dear," she said, "Was I ever in a mess! A card slipped out of my music book. I had to keep playing with one hand, lean over and pick up the card with the other, and then of course because it was a holy card I had to kiss it before I put it back in my book."

I am not saying that the Blessed Mother was not touched by this sincere act of devotion on the part of a loving child. It is not that she would kiss the holy card that is wrong—it is that she is afraid *not* to kiss it, and I may sound extremely sour, but this sort of thing leads many times, either directly or indirectly, to apostasy.

Far more healthy is the remark from an eight-year-old not long ago: "You know—I just don't like the pictures they make of the Blessed Mother." Pictures, in her mind, are pictures—and one is free to like or dislike them without any fear of dishonoring Mary. Pictures, manners, the length of her skirt, the face without make-up, the nails without polish, are not the substance of imitation of Mary. That, as has been said but cannot be said often enough, lies first of all in loving God.

IMITATING HER LOVE

Teaching a small child to love God is incredibly easy because God does so much of the work Himself. In baptismal splendor, the soul is free of any impediment, the dwelling of the Holy Trinity, and is awaiting the pouring in of revelation. With the knowledge that there is a God, that He loves and wants to be loved, and if we ask, He will teach us to love—with this, spiritual activity begins. We can teach our children to acknowledge the Trinity, to make acts of love, and to ask for the grace to love more, long before they are in school—and grace will accomplish marvels within them. It is as simple as finding a child alone with you, kneeling with him to say, "Let's think of the Father, the Son and the Holy Ghost in our souls, and tell them we love them, and ask them to help us love them more." This God cannot resist.

Again, love was the reason why Mary's will could so perfectly embrace God's will. One increases in love, one understands better how vast is His love, and His will begins to appear a manifestation of His love.

It was God's will for Mary that she bear Christ—that she bear Him in a stable and care for Him, that she nurse Him and wash Him and clothe Him, that she care for Him in Bethlehem and Egypt and Nazareth, weaving, cooking, washing, cleaning, teaching; that she be His servant, His mother, His confidante, His comfort. And it is when we hear Christ say, "Whatsoever you do to these, the least of My brethren, you do unto Me," that we understand wherein, after the love of God, our imitation and our children's imitation of Mary must lie. We must see Him in all men, and seeing Him, we must serve Him. Mary's way is the way.

WITH MARY TO SERVE CHRIST

This is why the imitation of the love: first, to see Christ in men. This is why the imitation of the virtues: to serve Christ in men. A child's imitation of Mary has nothing to do with superficialities and attitudinizing. It has to do with how one lives, and with whom one lives, from every morning to every night of every day of every year. Because the mother and the father, the brother and the sister, the baby, the neighbor, the bus driver, the school teacher—all of them are other Christs.

Gently, patiently, beginning when they are ever so young, a mother and a father explain this mystery of the Christ to be seen in each other. The most perfect, the most lucid exposition of it is, again, His "Whatsoever you do to these..." He said it again, another way, when He threw Saul from his horse and cried: "Saul, Saul, why dost thou persecute *Me*?" So there is Christ in Peter, and in Jamie, and in John, and Christ in Monica and Christ in Stephen. And Monica, who is eight, and is called to care for Stephen, to change his diapers and mop his chin, to dry his tears and butter his bread—Monica is taught that she changes, and mops, and dries, and butters for Jesus, and she does these things obediently, and humbly, and tenderly, and with love—as Mary. Monica, when she has to change a very soiled diaper (her mother in bed sick), will have to turn away to keep from retching, then asks the Blessed Mother (who knows all about diapers) to help her, give her the grace to do it—and *then* she will get it done.

TRAINING CHILDREN TO BE BRAVE

For Mary does answer their prayers and give them the courage they need. We had quite an experience recently, anticipating shots for measles. The little boys facing the ordeal had twenty-four hours to repair to the Blessed Virgin and ask for the grace to keep their mouths shut and not to howl anymore at the prospect of visiting the doctor. May that most pure Lady be eternally praised—she took them in hand, listened to their problem, and evidently talked turkey to them. We never had such heroism before! Every time anyone weakened there was a shout to Mary; we actually had *smiles* all the way to the doctor's and only yells for about *thirty seconds.*

I wish all mothers would try this, for I am sure it was a genuine spiritual experience. John Michael (who is four) is especially terrified of pain; for him particularly relationship with Mary must be made to be what it should be: quite virile, not sticky with mush and goo.

THE JOY OF MARY

Mary is perfect for children. She herself was a girl, raised Christ (a real boy), was far and away the most enchanting child God ever made (with the exception, of course, of Jesus), was *never* a bore, never a prissy mouth smooth-your-skirts kind of child, and was all they find glamorous in a woman. Beautiful—ohhhh! Adventures? bushels! Brave? the bravest! She knew a million stories to tell. She told Little Boy Jesus all about God (their favorite topic—really...) and on the score of *her* telling Jesus, can't you imagine the conversation when she taught God about God?

THE LOVE-
EDUCATION
OF GIRLS

Marion Mitchell Stancioff

**This essay concerns one of the most delicate topics. Parents
should read this with much prayer and consideration,
especially as the modern world has influenced this question to
the greatest degree.**

"From my own errors I have plucked one fruit; that is
measureless pity...for adolescents. For in our own time their
education is so little cared for that young people seem to
have no greater enemies than their own parents and teachers. These are the people who in a hundred miserable ways
deprave generous youths. Not only do they lead them away
from piety and study, but they teach them to live in pride
and luxury and lasciviousness. Open, Lord, the eyes, not
only of these blind parents and teachers, but of the stupid
ones also!..."

St. Peter Canisius wrote these ardent words of accusa-
tion in the sixteenth century. They are even more applicable
today to the great majority of persons responsible for the
upbringing of children. The word "upbringing" is, however,

a misnomer for the process to which our young are sub-jected. They are not brought up so much as brought low, not assisted in reaching their potential, but abetted rather in their own undoing.

Education has increased in volume as it has decreased in quality. Our children are being consciously educated in their cradles; their very toys are educational, with an almost doctoral gravity. What is the purpose of all this education? At what do parents and teachers aim? Few would dare maintain, in a non-Christian or only nominally Christian society like ours, that children are being educated toward membership in the kingdom of heaven. There survives as yet enough humanitarian liberalism for many people to believe that children are being educated for useful membership in society. How unsubstantiated is this belief anyone knows who has watched the rise of youthful delinquency and the flood of unhappy marriages. If the large majority of parents, however, were to analyze their motives, they would have to acknowledge—what some openly admit—that they are educating their children to get on in the world. The gospel of success, the virtue of ambition, a knowledge of practi-cal values, consciously or unconsciously form the basis of most modern education. "What does the world offer? Only gratification of corrupt nature, gratification of the eye, the empty pomp of living." And the education of Catholic children which should be unshakeably set against "these things that take their being from the world, not from the Father" is deeply corrupted by them. For what must be said of parents and teachers in general must—as were the words of Peter Canisius—be said of Catholic parents and teachers in particular. They are by far the more seriously to blame, for "they have no cloak of ignorance to cover their sins" of omission and commission. This is true especially of those in the wealthier layers of society, for they seek the most earnestly to conform with the standards of the world. In the effort to end for their children the rebuffs and disabilities which a low financial status had in this country so long imposed on them, most of our enriched Catholics dress their children as grotesquely, feed them as foolishly, entertain them as emptily, and altogether educate them as fashionably as their non-Catholic neighbors. Soon they are indeed as indistinguishable from these as their fond parents could desire; fond parents who forget how little this protective coloring will serve to protect them in the ultimate day. Let us examine some of the steps leading to this lamentable end. For present purposes I shall study but one aspect of education, the love-education of girls, not only because it is important but because laboratory conditions make it easy.

In the playpen parents and friends suggest the "boy-meets-girl" situation. At kindergarten mothers laughingly refer to every little boy as a potential "boy friend." The infant does not see the joke but hears the emphasis and begins to divide her playmates according to sex rather than to affinity. Modern psychologists have furnished solid evidence of what the old ascetics taught, that the innocence of childhood is a figment of forgetful minds. Bossuet in his treatise on concupiscence and Freud in his analysis of child-sexuality recognize this equally, and, though the hope of the one is founded in grace and the optimism of the other in psychoanalysis, both see the necessity to redress nature by education. What parents are doing, however, is not only to follow nature's bent, no matter how crooked, but to make smooth her paths, removing every obstacle upon her way. In their mental confusion they talk of Freud but believe in Rousseau. They people the world with complexes and fixations, with traumas and inhibitions, yet they treat their children as noble savages who can think no wrong. So the babies are given some physical training, a little intellectual instruction, and left with no moral direction at all.

Meanwhile our little girl, in preparation for her diversified future as (1) a Popular Girl and (2) an American Wife and Mother, is given to understand that the universe revolves around herself. She is trained to keep her hair curled and wear frills around her bare midriff. (These were designed for her elders in the movies, with the same purpose as the cutlet-frills of former days, to make the morsel they surround appear more toothsome and the whole easier to handle.) When, by dressing her like a diminutive follies girl she has been given the idea that she should act like one, she naturally tries her best to do so. She begins to imitate the women she sees photographed everywhere or reads of in magazines. Their smiles are so radiant, their lives so glowingly told, that obviously they must possess the secret of happiness. This, she soon finds, from every ad, is an open secret and its name is *love*; a special love that has clearly nothing to do with what the people in her orbit seem to experience but for which all the older girls are searching. She longs to discover this wonderful thing, attainable, curiously enough, only by an elaborate process which includes the conscientious use of various makeups, perfumes, garments, toothpastes and deodorants. She no longer enjoys her childhood but has a single-minded ambition to leave it behind as quickly as may be. Her greatest suffering is to be held back from entering the enchanted land of the grownups, where alone, she has read, love is to be found. Meanwhile she has been told at school some interesting but remote facts about the sexual ways of bees and birds which appear to have no relation to her own life. She probably has heard a few equally unrelated facts and legends about human sexuality from one of her contemporaries. Her mother has perhaps given her some information regarding the birth of babies which the child tucks away for reference in that unreal other world: her distant future. All this has nothing to do with her present life which flows on in its undirected search for the much more convincing and immediate thing called love. All the things she has been told, all this physiological information, is not much use to her, for it is still outside the realm of her experience. The one thing that is not outside her scope is love in its spiritual aspect, and that is the one thing she does not hear about. She is told nothing of the Cause of love: "He Who first created love," and so drifts on always further from her aim.

She wishes, therefore, to grow up and tries to do so by imitating not so much the flesh and blood grownups around her, but the paper ones who are around her just as much. She sees only the pleasures of being adult, and none of the pains and obligations and responsibilities because most of the adults behave as if they had none. Since full-grown people dress and act like adolescents why should children not do so? Some parents have misgivings and try to forbid this or that aping of their ways, but soon give up when they find their children secretly moping or openly rebellious. The papers some weeks ago published an interview with the wife of a political personage. She explained that her eleven-year-old daughter was permitted no grown-up privilege until she could show that a majority of her classmates enjoyed it. She had thus conquered the right to paint her nails and was looking forward to the day when she could use lipstick. The well-meaning parents' desire for their child's happiness had evidently kept them from following this principle to its logical and bitter end. If the majority creates rightness and if most people eat human flesh, then it's fine to be cannibals. This

majority-mania is a caricature of democratic theory and, if
followed far enough, may extinguish our liberty.

"But we don't want our child to be different," parents
will cry. "We want her to be happy. Being different hurts..."
What they are really doing is not only preventing her from
being hurt but from being happy by training her to exist on
a level where she will feel as little as she possibly can. They
do not want her to be capable of loving deeply or of making
sacrifices, but they want her to be loved deeply and able to
induce the sacrifices of others. In a word, they want her to
be "popular." Popularity is the criterion by which everything
is to be judged, the end to which everything tends, and for
which real sacrifices are often made. To be popular the child
must not be different, she must not be choosy about her
friends, she must be ready always to join them in their "fun."
One of the amusements the parents often suggest is kissing
games. A very devout and well-educated Catholic mother of
seven assured me once that kissing games are "good fun."
If the twelve-year-old finds no pleasure in a kiss there is no
point in kissing. If she finds pleasure in it, no precedent
could be more dangerous. I have seen charming, cultured
women at dances for their fourteen-year-old children turn
off the lights and heard them squeal when the tactless father
switched them on, "Poor dears, let them have fun a little
longer." Many parents think all this quite useful training for
the business of dating so soon to begin. These games and
parties help to overcome the natural distaste of the young
for the caresses of strangers. They help in breaking down
the instinctive desire to be inviolate, a desire as deep as its
opposite, if not eventually as powerful. The psychology of
yesteryear—which still holds the popular field—erred in
believing chastity to be unnatural. Chastity is the natural
atmosphere of human love, the essential element in which

love lives, its necessary condition. Unchastity is unnatural for it injures sensibility ("petrifies the feeling," as Burns admitted) and thus reduces the chances for happy love. But parents whose conception of love is radically vitiated can only see their child's happiness in conforming with social usage. They have kept a single standard in the confusion of these years: that physical virginity is desirable for their daughters. Short of that they either close their eyes, hoping for the least possible promiscuity, or else cheerfully permit it as the natural right of youth. There has grown up as strong a convention of promiscuity as there formerly was a convention of chastity. Society urges what it once forbade; and urges it for no fruitful purpose but as an end in itself. This preoccupation of our society with sexual things may be a symptom of infantilism or a sign of senility, but it is a certain indication of impotence. All things are approached from a single angle. Advertising is one long aphrodisiac designed to end in an orgasm of buying. Not conception but consumption is the fruit of our caresses.

Thus with minds conditioned by conversation since infancy and bodies conditioned before puberty by haphazard contacts, the children are prepared for the indiscriminate intimacies of the dating period. The sterility of this form of sexual experimentation has been pointed out by sociologists, who have proved that dating does not lead to mating. Dating is, as we have said, a sport rather than a part of courtship. It is more often, in the girls' case, a product of vanity than of sensuality, though it eventually comes to include the latter.

A Catholic girl of my acquaintance tells how she and a friend at the age of thirteen or fourteen, went out on their first date with two fellow students from the parish school. When the moment for serious kissing drew near the girls got panicky and blurted out as an excuse that they were both going to become nuns. They were "dropped cold" then and there, and for months, she says, not a single boy spoke to them. Terrified by this ostracism they determined to re-enter the normal school world again, and only succeeded by doing more than they had in the first instance avoided.

A Catholic psychiatrist tells me that she was consulted by one of her relatives who with evident anxiety confided that her daughter was not a "success," that she had once been asked down to a nationally popular dance and had never been asked again, while all her cousins were regularly invited. The psychiatrist, feeling that this was not a "case," made tactful inquiries of the girl's friends and drew the following reply: "Oh, poor D—? She just hates being pawed. She can't help it. But of course the boys think she's a lesbian and so they don't ask her out."

These cases are not so very exceptional. Often the necessary routine of necking is secretly distasteful to one or both parties, but such is the force of convention that they submit to it smilingly. She cannot offend him who pays (often at a great sacrifice) for her dinner by withholding what he has been taught to expect; he cannot slight her by failing to demand what she has learned to give. The formality which rules each phase of these encounters, from the first flower to the last farewell, is so rigid that beside it Mrs. Post's etiquette appears bohemian. The strict pairing off at young people's meetings, the unwritten game laws so sportingly observed with regard to each other's dates, prevent any general exchange of ideas, any true conversation, let alone any comradeship from developing between those who are not dates. And between the dates themselves there is the convention of a spontaneity so artificial that true expression of feeling is banished, and it is a great wonder that genuine love sometimes comes to life in spite of all.

Social convention, the desire for popularity, the fear of being different, do not succeed, however, in altogether blocking the Catholic girl's horizon. The religious instruction she has not been able to avoid has opened some chinks through which misgivings creep in. If she is at college she will find these doubts about the rightness of playing with the power and the privileges of love reinforced by some of the more intelligent and outspoken nuns. A very holy nun said to me once, emphatically tossing her veiled head, "Why, we here in our cloisters know more about love, and I mean human love, than most of these girls who play at it for years and never learn a thing about it, nor to value its work."

The Catholic college girl will find plenty of teachers who believe that "their" girls would never do anything wrong. If pressed, they would agree that perhaps a goodnight peck-on-the-cheek was exchanged at the door, but no more, and they do not seem to see the superfluity of that. They listen sympathetically to the girls' descriptions of their dates and patiently admire the dresses they will wear to their next meetings. These painstaking souls no doubt believe that this is a part of being "all things unto all men."

The girl will find others who, instead of teaching a healthy contempt for the ways of the world, a cheerful independence of outside opinion, and the unconventionality which is the heritage of the saints, never tire of repeating: "Don't be different. Try to adapt yourself. Do like the others in your class." These women would be deeply shocked if they knew to what activities their lessons in conformism were being applied by their preconditioned pupils.

If the college girl finds most parents and teachers closing their eyes to her problems, she finds other adults offering tacit complicity. One girl (known at her non-Catholic college as "the Icebox" because she does not kiss) mentioned to the woman doctor during a routine medical examination that she was having trouble with her gums, and received this reply: "How many boy friends did you kiss last week? One of them must have had a gum disease..." Another girl asked the fashionable doctor who was giving her shots for anemia whether the latter might be causing delay in menstruation. Without so much as an examination the doctor assured her there could be only one cause (*sic*) pregnancy, and added that although he did not approve of the ways of college girls, she must not hesitate to consult him, *etc*. This taking unchastity for granted gradually breaks down the resistance of the mind and accustoms it to accept any impurity.

Confessors in colleges are to be pitied. How far to go in the condemnation of evil without risking the loss of influence by excessive severity is their painful problem. Their every reluctant concession is brandished as a permission. Confessors have been known to grow popular overnight thanks to a phrase capable of "wide" interpretation. There are clerics who pride themselves on "frankly facing the situation," and they are much in demand as lecturers. A particularly popular one has tried to delimit the dangers of petting by dividing the process into a system of "zones," some of which are dangerous, he warns, and must not be entered until shortly before marriage. His elaborate instructions, given in all good faith before the tabernacle of the Lord, are thirstily listened to by girls seeking authority for their actions. They leave, triumphant topographers of sin, who know just to what point they may go, and refuse to realize that unless they wish to go beyond they had better not enter these zones at all.

If we agree—and as Catholics we must agree—that promiscuous caressing is an inordinate use of a God-given faculty, then we cannot "let it go." We are under the obligation to fight it. Yet how can we hope to do so successfully at this eleventh hour? We clearly cannot "fight it." It is the children themselves who must fight this battle. The parents and teachers who were their accessories or their accomplices must become their new allies. Let us look at the means.

In chastity as in all things education must be positive. We cannot expect children to value something they have never heard of. We dare not mention chastity, but dare to let them grow up unchaste. We must encourage the sense of inviolability that the Creator has put in them, cultivate in them a vivid knowledge that they belong body and soul not to Tom, Dick and Harry but to Him.

In their friendships they must learn to keep true charity. Although every soul is to be loved "even as ourselves," yet they will and should find themselves loving some better than others, playing or talking more happily with them, not for any external reason of sex or wealth or beauty but because of an inner compatibility given them by God. If there were more discriminating and articulate friendships there would be fewer confused and unhappy marriages.

We have found that in many cases it is not their senses which lead girls into promiscuity, but their vanity. From earliest childhood we should have been helping our children to overcome this evidence of human failings. If they were trained in simplicity, taught to deflate their own vanity, girls would not go on dates as if they were collecting scalps. They would want to go out alone only with tried and trusted friends. Their common interests would make conversation so abundant that no kissing would be needed as a substitute.

In most cases, however, we will find that sensuality does play a part and a very important one, in these encounters. This is only natural since God gave us our senses. Since He gave them to us for definite purposes, and since they are by their very nature more immediately compelling than our reason, not only must we enlighten children's minds as to their purpose, but it is normally prudent to avoid exciting their senses and to teach them to avoid doing so.

All this is needful and all this is nothing. For we cannot overcome passion with reason. We can only overcome passion with a stronger passion. We sometimes see an intellectual passion overcome sensuality with an arid austerity of its own. But the only sound conquest of an essentially fruitful passion such as physical love is by one yet more fecund. Otherwise there is a sense of frustrated life, a search for being, impossible to fill. There is only one love large enough to fill that need. We must awaken in children the fire of the love of God. Not a vague, sentimental tenderness for "Jesus mild," but the "love which is as strong as death." As Fr. François Charmot says, "Let us tell children from the outset that the source of human love is in God, as is the source of all love. Let us tell them early by example as well as by word that all love must be ordered to divine ends. We hear talk of 'sublimating love.' To sublimate is to draw purity from impurity. We have in the corporal phenomena of love a part only, though indeed a true one, of the elements which compose the total synthesis which is love. In it are contained elements of a spiritual order, even before any sublimation is attempted....Love has been made in the image and likeness of the Holy Spirit."

We will therefore help children to acquire chastity and charity and humility and simple prudence. We will teach them the Beginning and End of love, and the human love which is only a part of the whole, and explain to them its ordered relation. But chiefly we will try with the grace of God to awaken in them the flame of His love, which will show them all these things better than we can do and which alone can save them in the heat of temptation. "The only hope, or else despair, lies in the choice of pyre or pyre—to be redeemed from fire by fire." And we can only hope to make them believe us when we tell them this if we ourselves are truly changed, ready to be born again.

TEACHING CHILDREN TO PRAY

Mary Reed Newland

Teaching children to pray is, needless to say, one of the most important things a parent does. It is a most delicate time— and one which will affect the rest of your children's lives in a way almost nothing else will.

A joke currently booted about over the airways has to do with a small child saying her prayers and reaching, in the Our Father, the place where she lisps innocently, "And lead us not into Penn Station." In fact, the general attitude towards children's prayers seems to be one of gentle amusement, with now and then a little tear-wiping on the side. A sentimental subject and a popular one, with people who have their children pray. Strangely enough, a lot of people who never bother saying prayers themselves seem to feel that praying has a place in the young child's curriculum, that, for reasons very vague, it ought to be part of their early and most innocent years, along with fairies and Santa Claus and Nature Study and the rest.

Yet if there is a time for hard-headed approach to the problem of man's relation to God through prayer, the most perfect time is when the man is still a child. We lather the subject with sentiment and fail to see it in the light of cold logic. We quote glibly, "Unless you become as little children," and fail to see that in their very childhood, children are the most perfectly disposed to accept and understand God and that our job is not to marvel at the simplicity of their faith, the purity of their intentions, but to give them the means to remain as little children by training them in intelligent prayer.

Any prayer, if reverent and with good intention, is acceptable, but how much time is lost and how many precious opportunities passed by for lack of training in prayer. In an age when so much thought is given to proper feeding, proper exercise, proper clothing, proper recreation, all with an eye to insuring the future adult against a variety of physical and social maladjustments, it is tragic that just a small fraction of that energy is applied to insuring against spiritual maladjustment. Why should it be that the majority of men pass from the age of childhood intimacy with God into a long period where the relationship is barely a nodding acquaintance, then find themselves jerked rudely to their knees in the face of some personal catastrophe and forced to seek Him out all over again in their maturity? And the second seeking out is burdened with guilt of conscience, timidity in the face of long neglect and an almost complete inability to strip the mind of a lifetime collection of impedimenta and return to that state of childlikeness where there exists only God and the man, Father and the child.

At the moment of Baptism the climate is perfect for the beginning of a relationship which could be perfect. The Holy Trinity takes residence in the pure tabernacle of the child's soul, and he is at once launched upon his spiritual life. A woman once asked the nurse in the delivery room of a Catholic hospital, as she watched her new-born son trundled out to the nursery, "Please say an Ave right now that he will never commit a mortal sin." And the nurse, startled, replied, "Say, that's an idea!" St. Paul says we are called to be saints. The calling becomes a vocation as soon as the child is born. But the problem is not fundamentally the parents'. The business of being a saint, or trying to be one, is always an affair between the single soul and God. The terrible responsibility of the parents lies in their duty to make known the calling to the child, to start him as soon as possible on his journey to God through a lifetime, then through death into eternity. And the first and final steps are through intimacy with God in prayer.

The Sacraments are all-important, of course, but the Sacraments are God coming to us, and the reception of them does not necessarily guarantee that we will be saints. For two people to get anywhere with a project both must co-operate, and when one produces the means only to have the other refuse to use them, the project is doomed to end, at best, in mediocrity—even when the first party is God. All we can do for God can be gathered under one label: Prayer. It covers not only the act of praying but all our work, all joy, all sorrow, in fact all our activities, provided they are good ones, if we wish to offer them. The joke of it all is that the end of our giving is in order that He may give to us. So if we are going to run this race as though there were only a single prize, an early start is certainly an advantage. And if we are raising children to win the same prize, of all the provisions we must make for them certainly an understanding in the use of prayer is at the top of the list. It would be sensible, then, to establish a pattern of prayer for our children which would serve them without deviation, regardless of the particular circumstances they will meet, during an entire lifetime.

Too many people underestimate the ability of children to grasp spiritual truths, yet they will quote innumerable profound remarks their children make and sit back in a puddle of tenderness to contemplate them. It shouldn't be surprising that children make profound spiritual observations: their souls are pure, filled with the Holy Trinity, and the flow of divine grace into them is unimpeded. Granted their mental faculties are not fully trained at the age of four or five, but the relation to God does not depend on the number of hours per week spent in advanced nursery school, or the I. Q. rating, or the quantity of educational toys provided. And just because a poetic adult can contemplate God in the mystery of a blade of grass or the flight of a bird does not mean that the child's awareness of God in these same things is any less intelligent. With the child it is not an intellectual triumph that he sees the proof of God's omnipotence in all the things around him; it is a simple, straightforward fact, which is the fruit of the divine gift of faith in a soul filled with grace. Therefore, if we are wise, we will seize this once-in-a-lifetime opportunity and with the help of God's grace, try to equip our children with an approach to Him which will save them years of half-hearted, aimless effort.

We see, in the light of the various facets of our relationship to God, that we must address Him in a variety of roles: as the child of an all-loving Father, as sinner to Redeemer, as petitioner to the Giver of all things and as grateful recipient of blessings in abundance. Christ pointed this out in the Our Father and the same variety of approaches to God are evident in the Mass. Children, at quite an early age, are able to memorize the Our Father and the Hail Mary, but the chances of teaching the meanings of these prayers to any but those with unusual intelligence are remote. However, it is possible to use the general pattern of these prayers and give them a means of conversing with God which will include all the important points and still make sense.

The start is a salutation, of course, whatever form of addressing God is most natural. Then because getting one's sins off one's chest at the very first seems to leave the air purer and the soul freer to enjoy this conversation with God, examen comes next. It is important that the child be left to drag out his little aberrations of his own free will, and don't think they won't remember or they won't admit them. If the parents will make it clear in the beginning that the business of sinning is an affair between the child and God, and not an offense against the parent, it gives them the assurance that revelations in an examen are not going to be interrupted by remonstrances from mother or father. More often than not, a lot of minor mysteries will be cleared up at the nightly examen (for instance, which of our children was pulling the buds off the chrysanthemums—they were locked in mutual and honorable silence when questioned in a group). Then comes contrition, "I am sorry, Blessed Jesus, and *please help me* not to do it again." And right here pre-schoolers can learn that goodness is something which comes with God's grace, and without His help they are apt to do it again and again and again. Some days, of course, are very good days, and the immediate reaction at night prayers is to announce loudly, "I was very good today, God." On days like this, they can say "If I did anything to offend you today, I am sorry. I tried very hard to be good." And they are learning to guard against presumption.

Next, petitions. All the "God bless Daddy and help him with his work; God bless Mommy..." and *etc.*, fit in here. And after the most intimate associates are included, some under the heading "all my family and friends" for the sake of brevity, they learn very easily to include "all the souls in

Purgatory, everyone who has been so good to us, everyone in the world and please help the Russian people find God." This latter petition is apt to prompt some interesting discussion and some fabulous conclusions. Jamie announced one night, "I know why the Russian people can't find God. Because He's in our house."

Then comes one of the most important petitions of all. "Please help us all to be saints." To be a saint looks like a fairly easy job to a child, and they have a natural desire to be saints. Only the adult appreciates how hard it is and, looking back, wishes with all his heart he had thought of asking for the necessary graces every day of his life. We can train our children to—why don't we?

After this comes the break between the affairs of the world and this affair of the heart. "I love you, Blessed Jesus, and I love your Blessed Mother. And I thank You for..." each night a different blessing. The assortment of blessings and pleasures is legion and will include tractors and trucks and ducks and dessert and even, in the case of one of ours, "Thank you for not letting any motorcycles come in our driveway."

Prayers are over and all that is left is tucking in. But with tucking in comes the opportunity to plant a seed that will bear fruit very early in the formation of the habit of meditation, even though the child knows it, not as meditation, but simply as a kind of game called "thinking about." The choice of subjects for thinking about is limitless, but just for the sake of example: "Now before you fall asleep, you think about Baby Jesus and how He was just the same size as our Peter, just as sweet and funny, and how beautiful His Mother was. And you think of what it was like there in the barn where He was born, with only Blessed Mother and St. Joseph and the cow and the donkey to love Him."

It is particularly helpful to remind children that Jesus was just the same size as Peter at infancy, and the size of Jamie at four, and the same size as Monica at five, and so on; that He ate three meals a day, and helped His Mother with the dishes, probably, and probably had a cat to feed, and a garden to weed. There are lots of games for children to play which are in reality exercises in meditation. "Looking at the things that God made," is one which helps tremendously to increase their awareness of the vastness of His creation, yet makes the universe a rather snug place because on all sides they find it is filled with things He put there.

Children have such simple faith in the efficacy of prayer that it is easy for them to form the habit of praying on all sorts of occasions, occasions of minor crises during the day when affairs have progressed so far out of reach that it becomes quite obvious it is time to turn them over to God. They will voice their prayer aloud, matter-of-factly, and with the simplicity of the faith that is as a grain of mustard, they wait for the mountain to be moved. One spring day our boys discovered the top to the oil tank was unfastened and dropped two or three dozen rocks into the pipe leading to the tank. I froze, then collected myself enough to attack the delicate job of fishing out the rocks with an old fly swatter handle. They squatted around, very tense, and silent except for an occasional "Please, St. Philomena, help mommy to get the rocks out of the pipe." Of course she did. Yet our children are not particularly "pious" types. Nor do we stand around and prompt them. It is very easy to plant the habit, and their world is so much more secure because of this faith that God is ready and willing to help them on every hand, that calling on Him is second nature to them. I might say, also, that there have been times when some of our cynical and worldly-wise friends have been more stunned and edified by just such calling upon Heaven by the children, in the middle of an ordinary conversation, than they would be if pinned down for an hour's bombardment with learned texts by a zealous adult.

Add to these two other forms of prayer, and the child is equipped to "pray always." First, they love learning that work can be offered as prayer, and secondly, they adapt themselves quickly to the notion that suffering is a form of prayer.

Monica, at the age of four and a half, finished her after-dinner chore one night and went into the den to see how Jamie was coming along with his. Returning, she shook her head sadly and sighed. "Well, I guess the only people in this house who want to go to Heaven are Mommy and Daddy and me. Jamie just *won't* pick up the den and offer it up." And we have a small John who, at two and a half, will come wailing to the house with a stubbed toe or a scraped knee and as the offended part is washed at the kitchen sink, looks up at the Crucifix over the sink and snuffles, "For you, God, for you."

At about five, most children can understand the Our Father and the Hail Mary, so we have incorporated them into the nightly prayers of the oldest, along with the Gloria and several personal remarks addressed to her favorite saints. At mealtime they say, "Whether we eat or sleep, whether we work or play, let it all be for the honor and glory of God." And after the meal they simply say, "Thank you, Blessed Jesus, for the lovely lunch," and ask to be excused. Grace at table, of course, can be just about any form of address that appeals and serves its proper purpose, as long as there is some form of address used.

The morning offering is usually short, "I offer you this day as a prayer of love and thanksgiving, and I thank you for keeping me safely through the night." The "safely through the night" is not meant to imply, of course, that to die during the night would be the horror of horrors. I have heard too many Catholic mothers say, "My child says 'Now I lay me down to sleep, I pray the Lord my soul to keep,' but we leave out the 'if I should die before I wake' because I don't want my baby going to sleep with death on his mind." Of all the stages a man goes through, he has the least fear of death when he is a small child. Before he is filled with all the morbid notions adults entertain about death, death is a magical gate that leads to God and Heaven, and Heaven, of course, is wonderful. So it makes sense to a small child to be told, if he should ask, that dying in the night would be an elegant event because with God living right in his soul, it is certain he would be zipped right up to Heaven. If, however, he finds he did not die during the night, then it is quite obvious that God has work for him to do, and he will thank God for keeping him to do this special work.

These prayers, which take up much more space in the writing than in the saying, cover their entire day from morning until night, and they are set in a pattern which fits maturity as well as childhood. It gives them a sense of purpose in their conversations with God, supplies them with a motive for work well-done and suffering accepted, and the whole is geared to the common vocation of us, "who are called to be saints."

MOTHERS OF SAINTS

Sister Mariel, S.S.S.

All parents have the duty to raise their children to be saints. But how often we do think of those who have actually done such a thing?

Only a few months ago [on June 24, 1950], a little girl was raised to the altars of the Church. And her mother was there to see the glory of her child being shouted from the housetops. Happy but stunned by it all, the woman murmured time and time again, "Who would have thought it!" Her Maria, a saint! Her child canonized!

Such bewilderment is easy to understand. Think of the astonishment of Joan of Arc's mother when *her* young eagle took wing. Think of all the saints that ever walked the world and see a puzzled, anxious mother hovering near each one, in body or in prayer, not comprehending *but not interfering with* the mysterious work of grace in her child's soul. It is in every sense a fearful thing, a frightening thing, to be a Catholic mother, who must with every birth give a hero or heroine to the race of saints.

Non-Catholic mothers down the centuries have inspired greatness in their sons. Patriots, statesmen, great pioneers, how many of them assent to Lincoln's eulogy: "All that I am or ever hope to be I owe to my darling mother!" Good Protestant women and good pagan women have not been found wanting in efforts to bring up sons and daughters with high ideals and strong habits of natural virtue.

But the Catholic mother has an additional task. She too must build character in her child. She too must lay a foundation of natural goodness, of purity, truthfulness, obedience, loyalty, self-discipline; but if and when she stops there, as she does too often today, then she must sooner or later join the crowded ranks of the compromisers. She herself, more certainly than her child, can fall prey to the materialist outlook characterizing this century. And then we see secularism invading a home through its very heart, the mother, diluting or destroying the family's Catholic life.

So frequently Catholic mothers seem to fear that God's grace or God's Cross will manifest His action too clearly in their own children. "Look, Lord," these women say in effect, "I intend to give my child a Catholic schooling and not too bad an example at home. Can't that be enough? Please don't, on Your part, Lord, make Mary Lou *too* religious. Don't let her want to convert people. Or enter a convent. Don't make her *different* in any way from all our relatives and friends. And one thing more, dear Lord; don't make my Mary Lou suffer. Help me to keep her from suffering all her life."

We do not speak here of the obviously bad mother, like the one who gave her eleven-year-old son a cocktail party this past New Year's Eve. His friends were the same age and younger. It was so cute to see the little things drunk! We are forgetting also the mother who never goes to Mass, is married for the third time outside the Church, and who makes no effort to bring up her children in the Faith. She won't be reading this anyway.

It is the good, practising Catholic mother, who joins the parish club and works hard at the parish fair; it is she who has, in innumerable instances, mystified the casual observer by one day taking a stand between her own child's soul and its Creator, defiantly as any she-bear guarding a cub. There are no steps she may not take to interfere with God's plan or His work in the soul of her child. Because of the love that is due to her as mother, she can be the all but insurmountable threat to his or her eternal good if she so wills.

Bill is a young man who has secretly cherished since his altar-boy days a strong, clear call to the contemplative life of a specific religious order. At any time that he would allude to this vocation, his mother would become so upset that he postponed taking any steps from year to year. The draft made him face the issue squarely. Either he must enter the monastery at once or be caught in the draft and possibly sacrifice his vocation.

GOD (MOTHER) KNOWS BEST

Bill was to leave last Sunday for the monastery. His mother told him Saturday night that he could not leave until Monday because she had not washed his clothes. On Monday morning she insisted that he go down to the draft office and tell whom it might concern that he was leaving town. Unable to convince her that it would be wiser to write to the office from the monastery, Bill went down. He was informed that he would not be going anywhere, at least not where he had planned. Now he is in the army and his mother is content that he is safe from God's ways which were not her ways.

Instances of thwarted vocations to the religious life are so numerous they really do not seem out of the ordinary. An overprotective woman may understandably dread to let her boy or girl leave the warm home fires for the austerities of the *via crucis* she pictures in her mind within the convent walls. A possessive woman may understandably protest the completeness of the separation effected by her child's entry

into the religious state. The mother who fights tooth and
nail the supernatural desires awakened by Christ in the soul
He beckons is not commendable, but she is understandable.
Far more so than the woman who will interfere with and
impede her child's use of the means of salvation!

Such a woman is Mrs. Brown, who detests her son-
in-law. For years she has tried to break up her daughter's
marriage. From last reports, she has done it. For this end
Mrs. Brown has made novena after novena. Mrs. Brown is
a "good" Catholic who frequents the Sacraments, especially
since her husband died. Of course her daughter was married by a priest. Mrs. Brown knows that she can't marry
again; but if the temptation someday comes and if the civil
"marriage" is contracted, who will be the first to justify it?
Mrs. Brown. "The children need a father in the home, you
know." And didn't they have a father—their own?

Lucy Smith has a variation of the problem. She is happily
married to Jack and her mother likes him. Family relationships and attitudes have always been fair enough—until Lucy
announced that her sixth baby was expected in due time.

"Oh, Lucille! Not again—so soon! Really...!" Is it really
respectable, Lucille, to have a sixth when the Joneses never
have more than three? Lucy, in consternation, wonders what
in heaven's name her mother thinks she should have done
to keep up, or down, with the Joneses. And how will she
take the advent of the seventh, eighth, and if-God-wills-it
ninth grandchild? Mother never refers now to the coming
baby any more cheerfully than she would speak of a coming
World War III. But what would she have her daughter do?
The nursery jingle comes to mind:

"Mother, may 1 go out to swim?"
"Why, yes, my darling daughter.
Just hang your clothes on a hickory limb.
But don't go near the water."

Mother, may I go out to swim in the ocean of God's Love, trusting in His divine care, letting Him bear me up on the waves of His all-wise providence? Why, yes, my darling daughter. By all means keep up the appearances. Make your Easter Duty and what-not. Get yourself and the children to Mass on Sundays and all that. But at the same time remember God helps those who help themselves. You simply have to give some consideration to the world and what it expects of you. Don't sin exactly; but don't go off the deep end on religion either. There is a happy medium, a nice compromise, somewhere. Find it.

Valiant Mothers

Young Maria Goretti is today a saint among the saints, a martyr of our times who died for purity. What part did Signora Goretti play in the short drama of her child's high destiny? The girl chose without hesitation to die, brutally stabbed, rather than to commit a mortal sin. Before that choice ever had to be made, did the little Maria observe a thousand occasions when her parents asked in words or in manner, "What does God want us to do in this instance?" or again, "What does God think about this? What would He have me to do?" Had she noticed that her mother abhorred the little infringements on the "perfect law of liberty" taught by Holy Mother Church—the little lies, the little gossippings, the little bargainings with the Devil?

We can almost believe, without being often mistaken, that if a child chooses death to sin, the mother of that child would have chosen death for her also. In the long history of the chosen people of God three women who were mothers of martyred sons stand out like pillars of fire in the night.

The mother of the seven Macchabees lived long before the birth of Christ. She was forced to stand and watch each boy, beginning with the oldest, tortured and mangled and fried until death freed his soul. Any one of them would have been spared if he had but tasted a morsel of swine's flesh, forbidden by the Jewish law. The woman stood there tearless, urging her sons to endure and to die in order that they might live forever with God. When they came to the youngest lad the torturers wanted to desist. They thought that with time they could make the boy weaken by promises and bribes. Imploring her youngest not to fail the mother who bore him and to win his crown with the rest, the woman pleaded with the boy so movingly that he goaded the executioners on to dealing him the death of his brothers. Last of all, the mother was martyred.

Centuries later, a Christian mother as valiant as the Jewish walked across the scene of the martyrdom of forty soldiers of the guard in Sebaste, Armenia. The Church celebrates the feast of these martyrs on March tenth every year. All were chained in dungeons and beaten and starved for some days; then they were exposed all night on a pond of ice. To insure their death, the legs of the frozen bodies were broken. Melithon, the youngest of them all, still breathed after the smashing of his legs.

The persecutors piled the corpses at dawn onto a cart to carry them away for burning. They left Melithon on the bank, intending to revive the boy and then try more subtly to win him to the gods. They did not reckon on his mother, who had watched by the icy lake all night. She picked up the lad in her arms and staunchly followed the wagon laden with bodies. When the boy died along the way, she threw his body on the pile with the others "that as they had been united in faith and courage, and even in a common funeral, they might all go to Heaven together."

To Delight in Honor

The third great mother who consented to the death of a martyr-son lived later than the mother of the Macchabees but earlier than the Christian woman of Sebaste. If the latter two could will the death of their sons *because of eternal issues involved,* how much more readily could the Mother of God so will and not count the cost to herself!

But here we are talking of the heroic women, of martyrdom and the crucifixion of soul a mother may freely take for her share in the banquet of faith. These women are as far removed from the Mrs. Browns and the "hang your clothes on a hickory limb" mothers as a star from a fifteen-cent-store diamond. The pity of it is that, in the case of a materialist-minded mother, the bit of shiny glass started out as a star. And if it is not a star it is nothing—not even a real diamond.

Did heroism go out of fashion when the New Look of the twentieth century came in? G. K. Chesterton mourned in a poem the passing of those who delighted in honor from a world grown greedy and wise.

He would send the poor present-day idealists, born out of season, to Mary. Let them hand the trophy of "the broken heart" and the tribute of "the unbroken word" in the house of her "who bore the Child that brought the Sword."

And what is the Sword but Truth? Truth is the two-edged singing Sword, with the Archangel Michael's motto written on the blade: "Who is like unto God!" And the hilt is scarred with the single, grim word: "Sacrifice!"

Is it not from Truth that men and women have fallen since the turn of the century? Your grandfather and mine still had the wonder of it shining through their eyes, and we may well weep the dying of that generation. For only we shall be left—we who sneered in the nineteen-twenties at the falseness of Victorian sentimentality and then substituted for it the baser falsehood of materialistic amorality before the nineteen-thirties ended.

Every one of us is affected by the frenzied pursuit of the false. You and I who are the children of Light, the spouses, sons and servants of Truth Himself, we are all breathing in the exhalations of the advertising industry, for one thing, which sweats day and night to mummify our redeemed souls in the sticky cocoon of false needs, false wants, false hopes and false goals. Daily our eyes are blurred by the gray smog of the comfortable mediocrity into which we have been betrayed without a struggle on our part.

It is up to us, who eat the Body and drink the Blood of Truth made Flesh, to see our captivity in Egypt for what it is and to take up His sword and fight the good fight again. It is up to us to hand this sword on to our children; for we have put machine guns in their hands and atom bombs in their pockets while we rendered their souls defenceless by depriving them of motives for soul defence.

Response to Vocation

Grace will descend where it will descend, and the Spirit "breatheth where It will." It is the part of a Catholic mother to prepare the ground of her child's soul to respond to that breathing and that descent with the "Fiat" of Mary or the "Not My Will but Thine" of Our Lord in the garden. On such responses the world's redemption hung and still hangs, in a certain sense. Christ still seeks and claims His chosen, who will share His work or His suffering or both. And if He does not ask an extraordinary collaboration from every one of us, He does demand absolute fidelity. That is the minimum.

A child that has developed spiritual muscles on the self-disciplinary bars of fidelity to God in the ordinary run of his Catholic life, a child that has grown in wisdom and grace with eyes cleared by a thousand choices freely made between the visible world and the invisible, that child is the salt of tomorrow's earth, the "just man" for whose sake the Almighty One may spare us the scourge of His justice.

It was not for Maria Goretti's mother to know the designs of the Most High on her little girl. Designs there were, however, of a nature terrible and cruel in their accomplishment; but they were glorious and sweet in their final reward. If this mother had known how her daughter must die...? Any mother's instinct would grab the child from the cross.

That is the point where the Catholic mother can only look to the Mother who stood at the foot of the Cross and, like her, simply *be there*—transfixed by the seven swords beyond doubt but permitting and willing the will of God to be done in her boy or girl.

In a psychiatrist's office there stands a statue called *Mother Love.* A woman is kneeling with her arms around a boy on one side and a girl on the other. The children are facing the opposite direction from the mother, as if they are eagerly going on into the future while she clings to them and longs to hold them back in what has gone before. Each child seems to press forward and strain from the maternal grasp. And each child, with the hand that is nearest the mother, clutches at her breast as if tearing at her heart. Both children are oblivious of this pain they inflict.

The statue depicts merely the emotional conflict that the mother and child relationship must weather in varying degrees. If we look at it from our Catholic standpoint, we might see that the mother is holding the children back from the future *and also from God's plan* for their lives if not actually from God's grace. She binds them to herself possessively and she has already lost them. She would save them from life, from suffering. For the outstretched wings of the Cross she would substitute her own outstretched and clasping arms. She would keep them children—and she herself is a child.

Truth, fortitude and sacrifice are the weapons and wings of every Catholic. The ideal mother arms her child and teaches him how to be free. She accustoms him to the mysteriously sweet flavor of renunciation and to the joy of self-control. She holds before his mind the Face of the King for Whom his little acts of sacrifice or obedience or love are done; otherwise she will find she has reared a little stoic and not a Christian. Above all, this mother herself walks in the liberty of the children of God, with her eyes on stars beyond the stars, sure of the abiding Love of the Eternal Father. She loves but does not cling. And when her children leave her side she knows that she has set their feet on the road toward their heavenly goal. They are really free.

"Who would ever have thought it?" Her child, a saint? Why, she herself would have thought it—she, the Catholic mother!

RECREATION AND CHILDREN

Mary Reed Newland

Usually the summer months are the time when recreation is the prime topic of conversation. Mary Reed Newland, who lived with her husband and children in rural Massachusetts, shares her thinking on the subject.

Recreation means so many different things to so many people that this trying to sit down and write simply about "recreation" is likely to end up way off center. For some people it means what you do at summer camp, summer resorts, or clam bakes. And for some it means what you do on playgrounds, at nursery schools or on nature walks. And for still some more it means deciding between the movies, TV, dinner and dancing or a drink with friends, and so on. One man's meat is another man's poison, and to try to describe recreation as everyone sees it is impossible.

IT MUST BE FUN

For parents, recreation is as much a part of the spiritual training of their children as anything else, with one simple distinction: to be recreation, for a child, it must be fun. The other lessons aren't always fun, and some can be quite painful, but this one doesn't qualify unless it is. It isn't always fun for mothers, and in their human weakness, at the end of a long day of interruptions and messes and wasted time, they are likely to look at some of the most satisfying forms of recreation and see them as strictly a pain in the neck. By the same token, a child will sometimes look back on what parents have planned as a recreation and be either too tired, too full, too confused to get much benefit from it. This is not meant to be, however, a blanket disapproval of planned recreation or a finger-wagging at mothers who can't take mud pies on the kitchen floor, but simply a reflection on the fact that recreation thinking these days has taken such a specialized turn that we are inclined to lose our really delicate perception in regard to it.

The first years of a child's life are almost all recreation, or he won't get through them happily. From his point of view and for all he doesn't know it, learning, eating, discovering, inventing, all things that are fun and exciting, even humdrum but satisfying, are a form of recreation, which the dictionary defines as "refreshment of body or mind; diversion, amusement, as a pleasurable exercise or occupation." And the best clues to what recreation is for him come from him. Toys come first of all, at least things to play with, and here he often neatly evades what the grown-ups would have him accept as proper and fitting things. For example, every family's experience with the baby who, having unveiled all the Christmas gifts, returns to the kitchen to get out the pots on Christmas morning. After talking a lot but doing nothing about it, this past Christmas we bought our baby's gifts in the housewares department of the five and ten, and he had the best time ever with sets of colored paper cups, plastic measuring spoons, a plastic scratcher for scrubbing pots and pans, and a slightly off-plumb egg beater. Not that he did not enjoy the gifts people gave him, but children have an affinity for imitating grown-ups in their play, and to take advantage of it is to open one of the widest corridors to a child's learning.

WORK IS PLAY

Little girls love getting toy dishes and stoves, but they prefer being busy around their mothers' dishes and stoves, and until they grow wary enough to identify such carryings on with work (and, absorbing some of the attitude of a fallen world toward work, start to shy away from it) some of their very best times are had washing dishes, overseeing the cooking, and especially, particular joy, scrubbing the sink. They sometimes waste more scouring than they need, and hypnotized by the multiplication of soapsuds, pour out more soap than they need, but the meditations and musings to be bought for a nickel's worth of soap or scouring powder are rare and wonderful things, and if we really stopped to put a value on them we'd find such soul-satisfactions cannot be bough for a price. One of the most confounding evidences for the argument that recreation is sometimes intimately allied to forms of work is that remark often heard from little girls, "I love doing dishes at someone else's house."

Just because a kitchen is associated in our minds as a place to work does not mean that it is not one of the very best places to play, also. Just as garages and cellar work benches are, for little boys, very good places to play. If we have lost sight of this, not because we are stupid or insensitive but merely busy and distracted, we can regain the perspective by stopping to put ourselves in their places, to see, not the work schedule interrupted by the pottering child, but the pottering child who will soon be a woman. Considering the span from the cradle to the grave and the reason for man's being here, play that is imitation of man's work is really instinctive, and understandable, and God's way for preparing

His creatures little by little for maturity. And it shows that
God made man so that no matter how rich or how poor,
recreation depends more on what is inside him than what
is outside, and why, when to his parents the cluttered yard
and the bald spots on the lawn are anathema, to a child
they can be a paradise.

Sometimes it is the children of the poor who invent
the best recreations of all, precisely because they must invent them. Once, when we were really scraping the bottom
of the barrel, we discovered our boys—with nothing that
would qualify remotely as commonly catalogued recreational
paraphernalia—had taken an old mop handle, fastened to
it a piece of discarded hose, dragged alongside an empty
crate and on the crate was the sad, sad remnant of what had
once been another child's toy tractor. One boy was in the
crate, under the tractor, giving it a grease job, and another
was pumping gas in it with the hose fastened to the mop
handle. If we had qualms about what a child needs to be
provided with in order to entertain and instruct himself, it
was then we cast them to the winds.

EDUCATIONAL TOYS

It's so much simpler than the specialists like to imply. We
know of a couple who were determined their child should
have nothing but the most highly recommended educational
toys to play with—which toys are good and fun, but along
with them goes a kind of informal I. Q. test. They bought
a wooden mailbox equipped with different shaped blocks
which fitted into shaped slots, and presenting it, sat back to
calculate their small son's ability to figure out which blocks
went into which slots. He looked it over, took out all the
blocks, then turning the box upside down discovered the
master slot for removing the blocks, opened it and, willy-
nilly, dumped in the blocks. God love him, he was so far

ahead of them that one encounter left it behind—for all it was prescribed for his age and development.

So recreation, it seems, is a very fluid thing and likely to be discovered under the appearances of mere meddling, or messing around, or cluttering up, and is also sometimes quite recognizable as "play." Like all other things in life, it has to be subject to some regulation but at the same time not categorized and frozen in a set form. No one is suggesting, of course, that all a child's recreational peccadilloes be catered to or tolerated ad infinitum for fear of cutting him off from his play—or, like one family, the jungle gym be moved into the living room (it really happened) come winter and the end of the climbing outdoors season. It simply takes the same love and judgment (how easy this sounds!) to handle it as it takes to handle rewards, punishments, assignment of work, and all the rest of the parts of growing up. And like these other things, it has a definite relation to God and along with "recreating" should go learning to offer it to God.

RECREATION AND RELIGION

"You mean," Peter said, "that you can offer everything that's good to God? Playing? Even just standing still?" Even playing, just standing still, everything that is good, because everything that is good is a reflection of God's goodness and is a gift as much as those strange gifts of pain and trial He sends to perfect our wills. We receive the grace to have fun, just as we receive the grace to do other things. I think it was Monsignor Knox who said in one of his Slow-Motion books that he hoped his spiritual charges, offering up things for him, were remembering to offer a movie or two (cinema, he said) or a good cricket match, because he didn't want sour things only offered as prayers for him. And if we remind them often enough and lovingly enough, and after really good fun perhaps we shall help establish the connection between all forms of recreation and prayer. Otherwise, unless one anticipates a life of endless misery, it would be impossible to "pray always." At the same time it ought to establish deep in the subconscious the instinctive awareness of things that are fitting recreation as compared to those which are not fitting, and therefore cannot be offered as prayer.

There is a disinclination on the part of some people to "drag religion" into the business of having fun, when to ignore our relation to God in our recreation (while bleating constantly to Him about our work, our finances, our aches and pains) is the thing that is out of place, not the reverse. I have never seen a picnic or beach party spoiled yet by the acknowledgment, "Wasn't God good to give us this lovely day," or "If it weren't for original sin, there'd be no sand in the potato salad," and barring overdoses of out and out sermons, the fabric of detachment—seeing all things against a background of God—is woven step by step a little bit tighter with each acknowledgment that, but for His cloudless sky, or warm sand, or infinite foresight that would permit man to one day invent the hot dog, this party wouldn't have been half as much fun.

And at the times of the great feasts, outright religious recreations, including even mixed groups, are far more successful and satisfying—by virtue of the graces of the feasts, I am sure—than amusement for the sake of amusement. Many times it is the only opportunity for apparently religion-less people to acknowledge, awkwardly perhaps, a divine instinct deep inside which wants to be given a voice. The times when we have invited non-Catholics to celebrate the great vigils or feasts with us have been very happy gatherings, with—in the case of Halloween—the interesting discovery that when the background for the vigil is explained, the compulsion to indulge in even mild vandalism seems pointless.

COMMUNITY RECREATION

Because we are part of society, it is important that we think of recreation in terms of neighborhood and community recreation as well as in terms of family recreation. I know no parents who are deliberately anticipating bad entertainment habits as part of their children's growing up—only those who worry about the possibility; but too often all thought on the subject omits any real practical effort to forestall what is undesirable. It isn't an original idea, but neighborhood action is the answer; and recently several nationally circulated articles have told of communities enforcing curfews, party conventions, formal dress customs and so forth. Most of these accounts have dealt with situations already out of hand and how they were brought under control, but what is to stop the parents of the very young from establishing patterns which will preclude their getting out of hand?

We have begun feeling our way with a plan in our neighborhood, and even though there is wide difference in our various religious beliefs, we all agree that we want to raise wholesome, moral children. We want our children to grow up with a sense of recreation that does not limit itself to going to movies, listening to the radio, tearing around in hot rods or drinking beer and dancing. None of these things is essentially bad in itself, but the world holds so much more.

MOUNTAIN CLIMBING

Our initial step at a neighborhood entertainment was a mountain climb. We have on our land what is (by some people) laughingly called a "mountain" complete with trees, rocks, lichen, moss, fungi, birds, animals and fresh air. Best of all, it has a top which, when you reach it, you sit on and then you turn around and come down. Children from four to ten years old were included, with five mothers—we had twenty people in all. We all climbed, and after the climb we all ate, informally, coffee cake and cocoa. Not very world-shaking, but highly successful as a planned recreation and the good-byes were studded with, "Oh thanks—we had the *best* time." Living with a mountain ceases to be a novelty after a while, and under other circumstances I might have heard my children react to the suggestion that they climb it with, "Oh, mother—we already *climbed* it." But gather a group of people together and suggest it, and all of a sudden it's a terrific idea. So too is eating your lunch, or picking blueberries, or wading in the brook—when you all do it together. We haven't the time or money or transportation facilities to go off on elaborate forays in search of recreation, but we can work away at the business of establishing in our children's minds many wholesome forms of recreation by planning the simple things and getting them to do them together.

Successful group recreation doesn't seem to depend on the elaborate as much as it does on unity and enthusiasm, and if our experiences have been a measure, I think that city families in the same block or apartment house can make trips to the park, to the zoo, rides on the ferry, a trip to the museum just as exciting for their children as our (really prosaic) mountain climb was for ours, without spending more than bus fare or money for ice cream cones.

FAMILIES CAN rRECREATE TOGETHER

What's new about all this? Nothing—really, except perhaps our stopping to observe that more and more we have grown used to the idea that planned recreation is the function of recreation directors, community centers, summer playground programs, day trips and scout troops. And if we are convinced that this is so, then we have been sold a bill of goods. Somehow, some way, families—even families with one or two babies still in dipes, and fathers working odd shifts in factories—can challenge this idea that recreation for all of them together is no longer possible. If no other way, then by doing as a family I know did—declaring a "children's day" and leaving the chores where they were at a set time and simply doing things that were fun together. To neglect recreation, to consign it to the category of things "kids will do anyway," is like saying "kids will eat anyway" and not bothering to care what they eat.

And looking ahead to the day when in high school they will be driven by that overpowering urge to run with the pack—to neglect the opportunities to band together now in neighborhood groups and plan wholesome recreation is missing the one big chance to set the standards of the pack. Groups of Catholic high school girls all over the country have begun to establish conventions in modest evening dresses simply by, together, demanding them from designers. Whether it's strapless evening dresses, driving cars, drinking, whatever, something can be done and the earlier the better. Small children gather the strength and security for sound social behavior first of all from their spiritual training and their family life, but sometimes the best of them alone will waver before the pressure of ridicule and custom and "everybody does it." Supported by a group whose tastes are as wholesome as theirs, they stand a much better chance of weathering the delicate, dangerous years of adolescence and first experiments with maturity.

A COMMUNITY FAIR
Through organizations like PTA and others, essentially family organizations, there is recreational application to be made on even a broader level—the community itself. Our PTA is holding a Town Fair this year, the first in many

years, and almost the entire program depends on the fruits of creative family recreation, whether crafts, hobbies, flowers, herbs, art work or whatever. And for all the fun of entering the exhibits, the best fun of all is going together, with the mothers stopping to see the quilts and hooked rugs and the needlepoint, and the fathers the cabinet work and the metal craft and the chair caning, and the children to smell the herbs—taste them if they are brave, and discuss the flower show awards, criticize the art. Hard work, you may say, putting on a fair—hardly a recreation for any but those who will stroll through it. But not many of the people who work on it would agree. It is hard work, but in a strange way it is also recreation.

RE-CREATING GLADNESS

Defining recreation gets "curiouser and curiouser" as you try to track the meaning down, because it is so many different things to so many different people. For some it is work, for some play, for some study, for one lady I know it is caring for the altar and cleaning the sanctuary (most of her friends tell her this is a job for the janitor). Maybe the reason it is so elusive is that we never really look at the word and what it's made of—re-creation. What man attempts to do when he seeks recreation as a change and a refreshment from the weariness of his daily work is to re-create the gladness of heart of his first parents before the fall, when all the world and all of life was full of joy in a creation that was free of sin. Christ accomplished a re-creation when He redeemed us and poured His blood over a fallen world, establishing a society in His Mystical Body through which we could find paradise again in spite of the continuing presence of evil.

Outside of Him, all our attempts to recreate fall short, the joy is never more than transitory, the recreation rarely more than a diversion. But in Him we can find it—and maybe that is the secret of why the saints' lives were such a fusion of what we call by the common words—work, suffering, prayer, play—because they discovered that He is the instrument of re-creation, and in Him all human activity can become a recreation.

ON HAVING
BABIES AT HOME

This is perhaps one of the more controversial essays in the book. Some of the information may be out of date, but rather than a dogmatic necessity, consider it as a thought-provoking reflection on what has become today's standard practice.

The most surprising thing about life is that it can be suddenly so much over life-size. This knocks humanism out in the last round, every time. Huge ungainly events, earthquakes, wars, and floods, even those strange everyday occurrences, dying and giving birth, refuse to be fitted into the little pattern of our days in farm, factory or office. This really is not strange at all if we think of it. When we say "life size" we are thinking of human life. But if we remember where life comes from, who is its prototype and its inventor, we realize that the true measure and standard of life is God's, that His alone are the specifications and the plan.

Birth is something so odd and disturbing that it is really shocking, not in the now-forgotten prudish sense, but in the full sense. Being born is so shocking an experience, some specialists say, that it leaves a permanent trauma on the infant's soul. Giving birth is quite a shock too, even though the protagonist is an adult. Yet shock is part of our most important experiences; it is therefore not the shock itself we should try to avoid but endeavor to prevent any crippling effects.

First, this thing pain. It dogs us through life, yet we are taught almost nothing about it, neither how to suffer nor why we suffer. In the West the last few generations have been nurtured in a particular horror of pain. Almost, indeed, in a cult of cowardice. I know I was. Added to our natural teleological shrinking from pain, this conditioning makes us doubly vulnerable, more so perhaps than any people has been in the past. If pain seems the one thing unendurable, even nature's cruelties are more than we can face, and martyrdom is something beyond imagining.

Most of the young, however, have a healthy instinct for seeking hardship. Feats of daring and endurance appeal to them naturally. They like to climb, box, play rough games. In boys this taste is still somewhat encouraged by our softened society, but girls get almost none of it. Nor would they need these artificial difficulties if they were taught to face the pains of everyday existence. As it is, they are morally unprepared for the hardships of gestation and childbirth. Not only are they morally unprepared for pain, but they are intellectually rebellious against it. There is only one light in which suffering makes sense and if that light is hidden under a bushel they are justified in hating pain for being wasteful, wanton, savage. How can a woman take pain in a "relaxed" way if she is fighting it body and soul? If she knows its purpose, if her reason is reconciled to it, she will suffer no permanent harm. If only we could remember that we are mercifully being given the chance to "complete in our flesh that which is lacking in the Passion of Christ." If we accepted it with complete confidence in God's care for us, we might find that the yoke really is light, and our pains might become as easy to bear as those of the martyrs.

(I know a woman who unintentionally gave her dentist a shock. He was curious to know how she could stand without complaint the very painful work he was doing. She replied truthfully that she thought of Christ on the Cross, and that this made her own pains much smaller. This holds in every case. The dentist evidently thought she "had something," and although he "believed in nothing," he would keep coming back to this.)

Pain is certainly the most striking thing about childbirth. Pain and after that—joy. In the Old Testament God said, "I shall greatly increase thy pain and thy conception." In the New Testament He said, "A woman's heart is heavy when she knows her hour is come but then she rejoices that a manchild is born into the world." We have kept the first and let go of the second. We have increased the pain and killed half the joy. Women in different countries have told me of their experiences, have denounced the unnecessary miseries they have endured in hospitals, have protested particularly against the marring of their joy by the rules and regulations which surround the birth of a child today. I myself have had children in several countries. Never having been threatened with any complication which would have imposed hospitalization I had them all at home. I am not, therefore, an impartial witness when I plead for home deliveries. But I know of specialists in the field who are, and who plead as earnestly as I. Years ago one of the leaders of the nursing profession in the United States came out strongly for the home as the proper place to be born. In such a "progressive" European country as Sweden there has for several years now been a campaign against going to hospitals save in abnormal cases. The tendency seems to be growing amongst intelligent doctors and nurses as well as ordinary men and women everywhere. Let us see what the advantages are.

The Mother

It is usually assumed that the superior hygiene, the greater convenience (space, equipment, care), the "low" expense of the hospital put a return to home confinements out of the question. Under the present heading I will treat only the first arguments which directly concern the mother.

The low death rate amongst Patagonian mothers who pick up their newborn and catch up with their tribe, and amongst unmarried girls who have a child alone in miserable quarters and then clean up afterwards, has led a certain school of medical thought to argue that such activity is salutary and to try getting their unfortunate patients back to an almost normal life within a few hours of birth. They are wrong in their main contention, not realizing what a heaven-sent opportunity for rest a confinement can be to an overworked mother. (She should let nothing but dire necessity drag her from her bed.) But they are right about the negligibility of infection. We often read of women who have, while being rushed from comfortable homes to hygienic hospitals, had their babies in highly uncomfortable, unhygienic taxicabs. If a child can be born in a taxi, it can be born in a bedroom at home. Although it is true that, thanks to the high degree of cleanliness customary in hospitals, the incidence of puerperal fever has been strikingly reduced in the last generation or two, yet it is admitted that the puerperal fever rate only rose high when hospital confinements first became general. The danger of cross-infection, which in a hospital can never be totally eliminated, does not exist at all in the home.

This factor, hygiene, is therefore a compelling one only in complicated surgical cases. The same is true of space and equipment. Very little equipment is really needed. In those cities where children are still commonly born at home the pharmacies provide, at a reasonable rental, a drum containing the necessary things, already sterilized. The required equipment varies so much from place to place that I have come to look on almost none of it as completely indispensable. (In Italy an immense quantity of boiled water seemed to play a vital part. I do not remember anything like that volume being used anywhere else.)

Neither superior hygiene nor finer equipment nor greater space therefore make the hospital the "only place to have a baby." But even if all these factors were more important than they are, they would still be far outweighed by the psychological ones. What people call "satisfactory conditions of mental hygiene" can—in most cases—only be achieved in the home. When a child is born at home everything centers around the event. The entire household gives it its due importance. The mother's position is unique, her effort unduplicated, her achievement an undivided triumph. Noises are hushed for her comfort, her favorite foods prepared. Women have often complained bitterly to me of their arrival home after eight or ten days in a hospital, exhausted for lack of sleep. The routine noises, the calls for doctors over the loudspeaker, the lights, the nocturnal emergencies of their neighbors, the brisk washings and ministrations just when sleep seemed near at last, the half heard cries of the babies (and one always imagines it is one's own baby crying) keep many women from resting until they leave the hospital, and then they cannot do so because they have to begin to work doubly hard.

As for food, I have known a strong woman reduced to tears when faced by a tray of sauerkraut and spare ribs a few hours after delivery. Such a small factor as palatable food is quite important to a quick recovery of strength. Yet it is manifestly impossible in a hospital to discover the personal idiosyncrasies of each patient and cater to them. A home can and does.

Amongst other physical factors which have a high psychological importance is the matter of breast feeding. It is not at all simple. The mother or child, or both often, have difficulty in getting started. It requires much patience, which a good nurse must have, and much time—which no hospital nurse can possibly have. Breast feeding is often given up when a little more time or a little more *personal* experience on the part of the nurse would have made it easy. (This is where female relatives with their memory of family traits and peculiarities come in useful.) Not only is the formula struggle added to the young mother's difficulties, but tactless handling of this matter increases the danger of the most painful of complications, breast abscesses.

Quiet, restful conditions, food to personal taste, time to experiment with breast feeding are important to the mother's well being. But the purely mental advantages of home confinements are greater still. Even the bravest of us has a sinking feeling in even the best hospital. Although today disinfectant odors no longer assail us, we rarely hear a groan, and walls are tinted or papered to look like home, yet there is here a weight of collective pain which only the professional optimist can fail to feel. For illnesses requiring certain types of treatment this atmosphere is inevitable, and we must accept it. But childbirth is not an illness, and this phony-homey atmosphere need not be accepted if there is a real home to stay in. The nervous apprehension of what is about to happen is enough, without the added burden of that specific hospital loneliness. The moment when we are most at sea, feel most lost, becomes also, for purely artificial reasons, the moment when we are least surrounded by affection, most abandoned to strangers and to our own fears. It is true that the professional brightness of the nurse on duty shames us into tremulous emulation. But hers is a poor substitute for solicitude and tenderness. (Only a saint can keep true loving-kindness fresh through a hospital career. St. Camillus de Lellis managed it and St. Vincent de Paul's helpers did, but I wonder had they been plagued with as many precise rules as our nurses are, if they would have been as intelligent of individual needs or as loving.)

The lady having her first child finds herself suddenly in an unfamiliar, even repulsive atmosphere, alone, with all affectionate looks, no friends to ask little favors of. The worries of home are *not* left behind (Did I lock the door or not? Will he have enough shirts? I must remember to ask him tomorrow if this is over...if tomorrow ever comes...if I ever see him again). She is not only utterly alone, but what is worse, she is one of a bunch. Her misery is not made *less* by being repeated on every side, it is *multiplied*. These bizarrely reflected images of her suffering self show her all the possible facets of as yet unthought of agony. She would show greater bravery if those who knew her were there to value it. She would be more patient if by patience she could soothe her family's anxiety. She would be less worried herself if she could hope to get a straightforward answer rather than a professional consolation. She would have less the impression of having stumbled into Hell if somewhere she saw a sign of personal love, the one earthly evidence of Heaven. Sometimes such thoughts in the midst of their pains drive women to momentary despair, or into psychosis, which is a more permanent relinquishment of hope. Sometimes diabolical iniquity masquerading as scientific method is let loose on these modern counterparts of Job.

I know one sweet and very intelligent woman who came to New York as a bride some twenty years ago. She went to one of the best hospitals for her confinement. She still speaks with horror of that experience. *They tied her down* hand and foot. She says she was near madness then and the memory was so ghastly that she never had another child, and consequently ceased to be a practising Catholic. I blushed to think of my own good fortune, how I had walked the best part of one night—stopping only for pains to pass—first by moonlight, then in the dawn, amongst the flowers of a sweet-smelling garden, listening to the warm waves of the Black Sea lapping the rocks below, and how I had only gone back to my room when I felt like it, and had been free to bear my child as I wished. I thought of another time, in Italy. I had awakened in the night and phoned the midwife while the household slept, and had gone out in the cold spring night to unlock the big iron gate. The pale plumes of the mimosa brushed me and the orange gleamed faintly among their dark leaves in the light of a distant arc-lamp. The midwife scolded me a little for being out in the cold, and we both got busy preparing for the job. Work at such times has a most pacifying influence. I was considered a useful, responsible person, and, apart from the technical points, *I* was running the show. That, I think, is where the main difference lies. My unfortunate New York acquaintance was not considered a free agent; when they tied her down against her will it was for the doctor's convenience; *she* was ignored. The torture chamber technique to which they subjected her must have been quite popular at one time. I remember hearing that it had temporarily unbalanced the mind and permanently wrecked the marriage of a contemporary in England; but I have not heard of its use in recent years.

In the light of an experience of my own, it may *not* be ignorance but *fear* of displeasing the doctor by letting things get so far without him. In England the hospital atmosphere is brought right into the home. (In Anglo-Saxon countries the medical profession surrounds itself with an esoteric aura much more impenetrable than in continental European countries.) My first two children were born in England. With the first I begged not to be given an anesthetic until I should ask for it. But the anesthetist was brought, and I was anesthetized, and although pains were not very frequent the usual cutting and forceps work beloved of modern obstetrics was instantly resorted to. The next time, on the other hand, although I had repeatedly asked the nurse to call the doctor she was loth to do so as it was only seven in the morning. Then when she finally consented to call him, she realized the immanence of the child's advent and, reversing all her previous commands, yelped, "Don't push, don't push." Being still new to the game and overawed, I foolishly obeyed her, against my instinct and increasing misery, for an apparent age until the doctor and anesthetist had arrived and reduced me to the usual blackout. I afterwards learned that the baby had been born almost instantly. That was the last time I had a baby without knowing it.

From England I moved to the Balkans. Here there were a number of highly skilled surgeons, Berlin or Vienna trained. They preferred local to general anesthesia even for major operations and *never* gave an anesthetic in childbirth, no matter what the complications. Having by then been trained to regard an anesthetic as indispensable I was panic-stricken to think it would under no circumstances be available. The indifference of these doctors to the desires of the patient was as complete as that of the English doctors. For technical reasons some preferred to work on a conscious body, some on an unconscious body. They were good craftsmen as far as they went.

It was not until I had babies in Italy that I saw medicine as an art. The atmosphere there, no matter how pagan it may sometimes seem, is so deeply impregnated with Christianity that the patient's freedom, the respect due to the human person, is never forgotten. Gynecology was not the only department of medicine where I noticed this, for I had many dealings with doctors during our years in Rome. They did not need to talk of "psychosomatic medicine," there was no question of any other. One of our acquaintances from the Near East, doing his internship in a Roman hospital, felt this so strongly that he became a Catholic. "These people here even die differently from ours. We treat ours like dogs and they die like dogs. Here they are asked if they want a priest and they receive the Sacraments and die like men. Even the expression on their dead faces is different, nobler..."

The first words of my doctors when I went to consult them the first time was revealing. When I told the London doctor, rather diffidently, that I thought I was pregnant, he swivelled around in his chair to give me a bright look and a toothy smile and say unctuously, "Now isn't that just a *wonderful* achievement?" He was very kind, but he just wasn't natural about natural things. My Balkan doctor gave a bored grunt. My Italian doctor probably made no comment as I do not remember one, but just asked practical questions. My Russian doctor, when I told him I thought I was about to have my seventh child, said, "Of course you want to get rid of it—how many abortions up to now?"

After having been forced to have anesthesia in London and forbidden it in Sofia I had developed a sort of complex about it. A kind of nervous contraction of fear would grip me when the pains were coming on and prevented my utilizing these fully. My Italian doctor overcame this difficulty by simply giving my husband a wad of cotton and a little bottle of chloroform. When I felt myself contracting against the pain I would signal to my husband, who would quickly push the wad under my nose and let me hold it until the pain grew just hazy enough for me to relax, but not enough to prevent me from full co-operation with nature.

I was not only fortunate in having my children at home because I was spared the horrors people have described and under which I am afraid my character would have crumbled, but I was fortunate, too, in having my children at home where I was fully able to "rejoice that a child was born into the world." In the case of the first boy, born in complete unconsciousness, it is true, it took me several days for my feelings to "come to," and for me to realize that I had a baby. But when the second came I already knew how to rejoice. Those were the days when parents were not supposed to cuddle their children nor to pick them up except to feed them.

I nonetheless had the joy of watching mine in its cradle, and of course I held and fondled it too. I could show it off to my family and friends and see them admire it. I cannot quite imagine what it can be like to have the baby taken away and only brought at routine intervals. What a sense of frustration and emptiness must follow in the wake of the huge effort of childbearing! It is curious that women should have let themselves be deprived of their fundamental right to enjoy the presence of their own child. We claim every other less vital privilege and let ourselves be deprived of this. We have indeed sold our birthright for a mess of pottage

The Child

It is obvious that to the mother there is every advantage in bearing her child at home. How does it affect the child?

Hygienic precautions are normally taken in hospitals which, with the best will, cannot be taken at home. But *at home they are not necessary*. Naturally it would be unwise to have a baby in an apartment where someone is dying of tuberculosis. But on the whole, under ordinary conditions it is safer for the baby at home than in the hospital. The masks and glass cages are only necessary because of the higher risk of infection in hospitals. It is well known that newborn infants for some weeks or months enjoy a high degree of immunity to adult diseases. They are, however, extremely susceptible to specific infantile diseases. In crowded urban areas the chief cause of infant mortality was for many years infantile diarrhea. It is still sometimes epidemic and unfortunately often takes its worst toll in hospitals where whole batches of babies can be wiped out, cross-infection being difficult to prevent. This is only one of several ailments which can attack infants of the same age more easily when they are concentrated in one place instead of being scattered in different places as nature intended. We have already gone into the advantages of the home in starting the breast-fed child. Further, if the child is not to be breast-fed, it is as well that the family should witness formula experiments from the start to avoid later repetition of mistakes.

There are plenty of unpleasant tales about the treatment of infants in hospitals. It is difficult to check on these, as the principal witness cannot speak. Normally even a hard or bad-tempered person is less likely to make a baby miserable than an adult. However, risks are taken which no one would take at home. A neighbor of mine going to see his wife passed the babies' room just as one giggling nurse said to another, "I dare you to throw it," and immediately a small pink object sailed several feet through the air and was caught with the skill of a big leaguer and a great deal of merriment.

There is also the fact, too often laughed off as a legend, that babies may be confused. One of my friends tells me that she was happily feeding her baby when her eye happened to notice another name on his identification tag. The nurse went in search of her child and after some time found him with no identification mark. These children were indistinguishable except by weight. Another friend, a doctor, was proudly taking his wife and son home, when the nurse in the elevator asked if she might check his number again. It was someone else's baby and none of them had seen the difference.

Some acquaintances of ours in a small Swiss town had twin boys. When we knew them they were just beginning to go to school, nice kids both of them, though very unlike in many ways. One day at a rally in which all the schools in the town took part, the spectators who knew the family were struck by the appearance of *three twins* in the ranks of children, two of whom were identical. The two horrified sets of parents discovered that the "third" twin had indeed been born in the same hospital on the same day. The parents of the twins were French-speaking Catholic intellectuals. The parents of the third child were German-speaking Protestants of very rudimentary education. The discovery of the error created an insoluble dilemma for them all, a problem which could never have existed had they been born at home.

THE OTHER CHILDREN

Mothers of families who have their babies at home have to find someone to take care of the older children. That difficulty exists equally when they go away to a hospital. If there is enough room and the possibility of getting a friend or relative to come and look after them at home, it is far better not to send them away. If that is inevitable then it must be presented as an adventure lest it be resented as an exile.

Very sensitive children often regard their mother's going to the hospital "to get a new brother or sister" as a kind of infidelity to the pattern of the home, a deliberate preference for an "outsider." If the sudden multiplication of life is *in* the home, the new life in the old setting is a valuable discovery for the child's mind. It is a particularly good experience for older children as it permits them to learn naturally what they would later learn from textbooks.

Mothers nowadays show their children, not the friendly room at home, but the cold administrative-looking hospital building where they were born. This building is either quite strange to the child and will leave a puzzle in its mind, or it is linked with some painful memory such as a tonsillectomy. Birth becomes associated with strangeness or with terrible surgical impressions, instead of taking its place in the scheme of things, like the ripening harvest and the changing seasons.

THE HUSBAND

In Anglo-Saxon lore we are familiar with the anxious husband pacing nervously up and down before a closed door, waiting for another man to bring him the news of his child's birth. This figure is practically unknown in Latin countries because, unless the husband is hopelessly selfish, he is in there helping. He has plenty to do. He has to encourage his wife by words and looks, be ready to hold her hand and make himself useful in a practical way too. This cooperation, this minute-to-minute knowledge of events racks the nerves far less than floor pacing, door gazing, and chain smoking. It is better not only for his nerves but for his character.

The nervous agony of waiting inactive and ignorant ends up by making a man almost as sorry for himself as for his wife. If he is with her he will forget himself and think only of her and of their future child. After the child is born he will have quite a bit to do, and if mothers, sisters or aunts are scarce he may even have to do some housework. He may have to cook some little thing his wife likes and even if it is not up to hospital standards his wife is more likely to try and eat to please him. He too can rejoice over the child that is born into the world. He can glow with pride over his baby—or settle his anxieties about it—by looking at it whenever he wants instead of waiting for certain times, which he cannot always make because of work, then seeing his flesh and blood under glass in the hands of a stranger. The husband, the "forgotten man," should take back his part of responsibility just as the wife should be allowed to take back hers.

The Family

We cannot stress enough the uniqueness of each birth and death in the world. It is when man loses sight of that uniqueness that he creates concentration camps and orders mass executions. While each mother and each child is the only one of its kind, in our eyes as it is in God's, its care will be safe in our hands. This lumping human beings together is one of Satan's wiliest ways of devaluating the individual and particularly the family. Because indiscriminate grouping is unpleasant we are to believe that even natural grouping is unnatural. These hospital scenes of group deaths and group births are highly unnatural. Like the group death ordered by Herod they involve a massacre of the innocents, a destruction of some of those natural instincts which are always being invoked by those who chiefly destroy them. We cannot expect people to develop a healthy family instinct if they start off like this. This is the way to produce party members, not family members. If "cruel Herod" fails once more, as he failed when he pursued the Holy Family in his effort to exterminate the Child, it is a further testimony to the survival power of all that is made in the image of God.

The Doctors

We have now added up the advantages to various people of childbearing in the home—to the mother and to the child, to the older children and to the father, to the relatives and to family life as a whole, and consequently to the community as a healthy group of healthy families. We have not examined its effect on the doctor. But all these advantages would certainly outweigh any possible disadvantage to the members of a single profession. What are these disadvantages? Obstetrics is after all only a part of gynecology, and gynecology only a part of medicine. The profession would not suffer seriously even if babies were born without medical aid—which is far from being anyone's desire. One is only too glad to have the reassuring presence of a doctor when the time comes. (I had not called my doctor for my second confinement in Italy, being rather low in funds. But he had heard of it through the midwife and came anyway, refusing to be paid, and I have rarely been as delighted to see anyone.) There is no reason why a doctor would suffer financially for attending a patient in her home rather than in a hospital. The fee could be the same either way. There is certainly greater inconvenience to the doctor in attending scattered patients instead of having them corralled for him. There would be a need for a small increase in the number of doctors. More young doctors could get started, though they might make slightly less per year. If the doctor could get to a confinement in horse and buggy days there is no reason why he should fail to get there in dynaflow days.

The Midwife

The midwife might perhaps claim—more honorably for the female sex than the traditional claimant—to practice the oldest profession in the world. Paradoxically enough, her work was respected and she throve until the age of feminine ascendency, when suddenly she was thrust from her calling. This job where personal experience is invaluable, where direct knowledge of the sensations and symptoms cannot be *replaced* by any amount of memorized book learning, has become the prerogative of men and unmarried women. Whoever heard before of a mid*maid* instead of a mid*wife?* This novelty neither makes sense nor inspires confidence, yet so much depends on the woman assisting at a delivery.

If we are to start home confinements again, everything will hinge on the midwife. She must not only be well trained in the theory and well grounded in the practice of her work, she must also be naturally intelligent, having what used to be called "mother wit." She must be simple and kind. I have known some wonderful ones who had brought great numbers of children into the world, with so much skill that they had no need of the snipping and sewing technique men in their haste sometimes use without need.

The best I have known were a Russian and an Italian. (I am glad to be able to bear this testimony to a suffering people too often confused in men's minds with the tyrants who rule them. The best trained nurses I have known were all Russians. Not only were they kinder, more thoughtful, more self-effacing, more perseveringly conscientious, quieter and more alert, but their training seemed to have been more thorough than that of other nurses and they had, besides, an understanding of medicine, a "medical sense" such as I have not known many doctors to possess.) I know that New York had an excellent school of midwifery until it was obliged to close down a few years ago, and its graduates were forced out of their profession by legal discriminations against them—ingloriously lobbied for by doctors. If women want to have their children born at home they must see to it that other women are trained to assist them.

EXPENSE

Early in this article I mentioned expense as being one of the reasons put forward against having children at home. It is in most cases the decisive argument. People are inclined to say wistfully, "Only very wealthy people can afford to have babies at home." Ours is indeed a poor generation if only the very wealthy can indulge in what every workman's wife could afford fifty years ago. If a reasonable system were adopted, having babies at home would be within the reach not only of the rich and medium-rich but of the poor and semi-poor; not perhaps within reach of slum dwellers, since even a hospital is possibly—though not certainly—to be preferred to their one-room flats. But no mother who has at her disposal running water, a stove and a second room need go to a hospital—provided she can enlist the cooperation of a doctor or nurse. As things stand now the nurse comes for eight hours, goes away just when she is needed and costs a great deal. I came across a system in Italy which struck me as being both cheap and good for all concerned. The nurse (midwife) having assisted at the delivery, with or without a doctor (most of my friends had a doctor for their first confinement and managed without for the others), cleans up and then leaves the patient to the care of her family. She returns morning and evening for a week or two according to the needs of the patient. She washes her, checks up on her and the baby and thus spends an hour or two each day at each home, her visiting hours being planned according to the topographical distribution of her patients. She often works with an assistant who is learning the work and who can take over the daily wash and check-up if the midwife is kept at another confinement. Her fees are far more moderate than the cost of a hospital room, yet she has enough patients concurrently to make a very decent living. The non-technical care, such as food and slops, is taken on by the family and costs nothing. It is good training for them in Christian charity, and in a family worth its salt they are all glad to do it. A wealthy woman, or a very sick one, who would have a private nurse in a hospital would have one at home for the same fee. There is everything to be gained and nothing to be lost by adopting an analogous system.

The midwife would be easy to revive provided the doctors were willing. The doctors will be willing only if the women persuade them that they want to have their babies under their own roofs. Some doctors have already begun—I know of one doctor in a midwestern state and another in an eastern state whom a crowd of grateful patients loudly praise, and who bear witness to the excellent results of home confinements. May their numbers be multiplied, that women may rejoice again when a child is born into the world.

When man gives up the God's-eye view of himself he develops an ant's-eye view or worm's-eye view of himself. He sees only the detail, no longer the whole scene. The doctor sees only obstetric hazards, the nurse only hospital rules, the woman only housekeeping neatness and fears something in her pretty little home may get messed up by a thing of such magnitude as birth. The whole is lost in the parts and we cannot see the wood for the trees. Yet the welfare of the whole is bound up with the welfare of the parts. God has not made them to work one against the other but in harmony. The good of mother and father and children, of grandparents and friends, of the family as a group and the community as a whole is the same. In the light of God and the laws of nature ordered by Him lies our own good. It is never too late to begin to be right.

BREASTFEEDING

Mary Reed Newland

Breastfeeding is again becoming the accepted thing in some circles. Since it might still seem bizarre to some, we asked Mrs. Newland, the mother of six children, to discuss it in *INTEGRITY*.

Exactly why and when Breastfeeding ceased to be the accepted manner of feeding infants I have not had the time to discover, but it must inevitably have begun to lose vogue with the emancipation of women—that emancipation which freed them from so many of the obligations and privileges of wife and motherhood, which dragged them out of their kitchens and into their offices, out of their nurseries and around their bridge tables.

Whatever its beginnings, it is plain to see that as birth control became socially more acceptable, the natural (as contrasted with unnatural) and obedient use of the procreative powers and the resulting large families became socially less acceptable. There finally hovered about the reputations of fertile parents an aura of the animal-like—it apparently failing to occur that the deliberate failure to reproduce was no measure of continence, or contrarily that the very cycles of baby-bearing impressed continence periodically upon the obedient and fertile. In a perverted way, deliberate sterility became synonymous with chastity, and fertility with a kind of carelessness or promiscuity in marital relations. Following in logical sequence, all the normal attitudes and practices appending to the business of baby-bearing suffered the same perversion, and Breastfeeding among other things ended up being socially repugnant.

How Ridiculous

Viewed from the vantage point of the Creator, bottle-feeding must look not only unnecessary but a little ridiculous. It is only beginning to occur to us how ridiculous. After moving along for thousands of years using the bodies God gave us to feed our infants a food that is nature-made for them, that is impeccably clean, that is available at a moment's need, that is dispensed in the most psychologically happy manner, we thought for a brief half century or so to improve on God's way by inventing a glass bottle only vaguely resembling the human breast, equipping it with a rubber nipple which now dispenses, now does not, and filling the bottle with food that God intended for mother cows to feed to baby cows. Sounds silly, doesn't it?

Howsoever, here we are with many mothers bottle-feeding their babies, with many who honestly cannot breast-feed, who are too nervous, too ill-nourished, or in whom the repugnance to Breastfeeding has become so deeply ingrained that it is a psychological impossibility. And I do not intend to scoff at my formula-feeding sisters. Many would leave the ranks, I am sure, if they were given only a little encouragement. There is probably little that is deliberately malicious in the discouragement met on all sides by would-be nursing mothers, but whatever the reasons, unenthusiastic doctors and nurses account for as many failures in the Breastfeeding department as do nervous temperaments and difficult babies.

INEVITABLE DISCOURAGEMENT

I was told flatly that I could not nurse my first baby because he wasn't learning to nurse fast enough, was losing weight too fast, the quality of the milk was not up to par, he wasn't happy nursing, and he awoke frequently between feedings and cried in the hospital nursery so had to be fed a formula. It was all very convincing, and like a good obedient girl I accepted the verdict, wept copiously, wondered why after so many earnest prayers Jesus and Mary had not pulled the attempt off successfully for me, and went home resigned to be a formula-feeding mother.

By the time the next baby was on the way we were very poor, and that meant, among other things, that there wasn't going to be enough money to buy extra milk for the new baby. If only I could nurse. So once again we started to pray that in spite of the first failure the second time things would go better. Things did, and I think that probably along with the prayers it was the dire need and the determination that made the difference. Once again I was discouraged but this time, not quite so wide-eyed and gullible, I insisted that both the baby and I be given a chance to work it out. It never did work out there in the hospital. But it finally worked out at home, and then it became quite clear that of course I could breast-feed, and could have done it with the first baby. The determinant in the failure had not been me or baby, but the unnatural four-hour schedule in the hospital, the impatience of the nurses, who had little or no time to be wasted trying to fit the newborn's erratic feeding schedule to their own busy day, and the general attitude of tongue-in-cheek which greeted the announcement of a would-be nursing mother in their midst. I do not entirely condemn the discouraging doctors and nurses. They are as firmly enmeshed in the social system we have cast as the rest of the world, and as things stand now only a few hospitals are equipped to handle the procedure whereby mother and baby are kept side by side and baby may eat whenever he wishes. Until this is universally possible, mothers who want to breast-feed will continue to struggle against the artificial four-hour hospital schedule unsuccessfully, and the only thing to do is to hang on to your convictions until you get home. So much for discouragement at the hospital.

EMBARRASSING?

There are some mothers who resist Breastfeeding because they are afraid it will not fit into the pattern of home and neighborhood life and will net them more embarrassment than satisfaction. I remember a young mother who gave this as her excuse for not Breastfeeding. Her father-in-law lived with them, and she was sure trying to nurse her baby would be more humiliating than anything else, with her menfolk forever walking in on it, embarrassing her and being embarrassed, and she herself completely retired socially until the baby could be weaned. She was finally coaxed, however, to agree to nurse her baby for the first two weeks, even though unconvinced that her feeling about nursing would change. It did not take two weeks for it to change, but two days; and after two days she smiled and said, "I see what you mean now. There's something about nursing a baby, isn't there?"

CONTINUING CREATION

There is something about nursing a baby—something that is communicated to the whole family—and it is something that is predominantly spiritual, for all the physical form it takes, because it is an extension of the act of creation. To make a baby takes nine months of walking sacramentally, with every step dedicated; nine months of mystery and miracle where a seed so tiny it cannot be seen by the naked eye can achieve form and shape and intelligence and soul.

All this comes to be by the power of God but made from the substance of our own flesh, until at the end in an act so great that it has ramifications in eternity, a person is born, another immortal.

But this is only the beginning, and the act of creating continues. The baby is not meant to be snipped free from his mother like a paper doll, suddenly to take up existence totally independent from her. He has been growing for nine months, he must continue to grow, and there is the continuance of creation in each new cell, each new eyelash, each new tear.

Animal babies, bird babies, insect babies, within a few hours or days of their birth are able to survive by themselves—but not human babies. More than any other creature the human baby is totally helpless and at his mother's mercy. And it would be utterly illogical if this dependence of the infant upon his mother were not provided for by God. First of all, and almost immediately, there is an increased awareness in the mother, a maternal instinct aroused to such delicate perception that one can almost sense when a baby is in need. I have read somewhere, and whether theory or isolated fact it is entirely reasonable, that with the coming of the mother's milk there is a glandular activity which accounts for this increase of awareness. Surely it sounds like the kind of thing God would do, Who is able and has performed such miracles of intricate maneuver in the body already. And observing first His great care to prepare the mother instinct, it follows that the further unfolding of the physiological aspects of His plan are equally to be marvelled at. He has created for the mother a body which not only bears this child but also feeds it, and the act of Breastfeeding a child is an intimacy second only to the carrying of it.

So the tiny creature who lay tucked so snugly away in the darkness of the mother's body is now weaned a little away from her, but not too much or too fast from his warm retreat, his sweet closeness to his mother. His growing up will be daily, a step after a step away from her, but God is incredibly gentle, His timing is divinely perfect, and the transition from the womb of the mother to her arms, to feed at her breast, is designed in tenderness and divine mercy.

There is another marvel to be observed here. Before the mother's breast begins to manufacture milk, it produces a substance called colostrum, which is an aid to flushing out the last residues from pre-natal life which remain within the baby. Does it not seem a senseless omission—failing to use what God has designed for the baby's best good?

THE MOTHER'S NEEDS

The mother has many needs too, after the birth of her baby. First of all she needs rest, along with activity—a nice proportion of each in order to regain her strength, her stamina, her equilibrium. One plans to rest, but once home from the hospital there is so much to do, such chaos to right, that rest is bought too dearly and often foregone entirely. God is not whimsical, but He is wise, and knowing this side of woman well He has contrived a situation following birth in which the mother *must* rest. Anyone who has had a baby will agree that along with having a few good cries for herself, one of the things mothers invariably do is overestimate their strength. The swift rush of energy is soon drained and nothing looks so good as a chair to collapse in.

Now consider the pattern of the baby's hunger. It does not facsimilate the rigid four-hour schedule of the hospital. It is a pattern of crying, nursing, dozing, then crying, nursing, dozing, and it makes very good sense. The infant is tiny, he has never eaten this way before, in fact he has never known hunger before; he is weak and is incapable of sustaining for very long any energetic undertaking. Even the act of eating burns his meager energy and with just a little warm food in him, he will doze off—his way of resting and regaining his strength in order to awaken and cry again for food. Contrast the wisdom of an Almighty Father Who provides warm, sterile, especially appropriate food at whatever intervals baby demands it, together with a period of required rest for the mother, who must sit or lie down in order to feed her baby, with the earnest but unnatural procedure that requires heating and reheating a bottle and a recurring battle with the inclination to prop the bottle and get in an extra few licks on the housework while baby is busy feeding. I have always thought it a little like the closed barn door with the horse out to hear admonitions about picking baby up and cuddling him when he has his bottle, in order to approximate the intimacy of Breastfeeding. It makes so much better sense to breast-feed.

There is another physiological advantage to Breastfeeding which benefits the mother, one that grows out of the sensitive relationship between nursing and the return of the uterus to its normal position and size. This part of the recuperation after childbirth varies with individuals, but roughly speaking it takes the full six weeks of the post-partum period before the uterus is returned to normal and the mother's internal anatomy is as it was before. The return to normal is much more rapid with Breastfeeding mothers; once again we see a deliberate feature of the divine plan.

And wed to all these wonders still one more, the unerring instinct with which the baby—without being coaxed more than once or twice—knows why he is being held to his mother's breast, and weak as he is, knows how to suck.

It could never be explained to him—but it need not be. He comes already knowing.

Why the Stigma?

Perhaps it is here, at the moment when the baby actually begins to breast-feed, that the largest share of objection is registered by mothers, either frankly aloud, or secretly to themselves. There is a stigma attached to it, hard to explain. Somehow it doesn't seem quite what a gentlewoman would do—especially not in front of anyone. In fact, with some people there is an open aversion to it as though it were animal-like. We dismiss these objections with one reminder: the Mother of God nursed *her* Baby, than whom there was no more gentle gentlewoman.

It may not be socially acceptable to nurse one's child in public, but when the same society which frowns on this accepts without a tremor the wholesale denuding of young women on the beach, on the dance floor, and in the entertainment world, it is silly even to look to society for a rule. Mothers do not ordinarily go about nursing their babies in public unless it is absolutely necessary, but when it is, it is usually under conditions which provide an inspired frame for what is obviously a very fundamental and womanly act. I remember several years ago (following, I believe, the devastation of the Ohio floods) seeing a photograph of a mother sitting on a pile of rubble, bereft of her home, her belongings, possibly even some of the members of her family, serenely nursing her baby. It was nationally acclaimed as the most beautiful news photograph of the year. And it was because she was performing her function as mother under conditions that demanded heroic fortitude that the shot had such great beauty.

A Holy Act

The difference between mere nudity and the partially bared breast of a mother who nurses her baby is simple: the latter is holy. Discretion calls for privacy if it is possible, but a sense of the holiness is communicated even when privacy is not possible and not only father and the children but sometimes even their friends wander in while the youngest member of the family is having his lunch. Children, and even neighbors if they happen to be in and out a lot, accept it quite simply for what it is—the feeding of a child the way God meant it to be fed. Familiarity with it is obviously what God wills for the family, and it is not the familiarity which breeds contempt, but rather a deeply rooted understanding of the whys and wherefores of feminine anatomy and design.

Not long ago a little boy wandered in where I was nursing our new baby, and after his initial start, gasped:

"What is he *doing?*"

"Why, he is having his lunch, Christopher. Have you never seen a baby fed by his mommy before?"

"No." And he pondered deeply a few minutes watching us. Finally he turned and made his way down the hall with these words, very distinct:

"So that's why mommies have bosoms."

Wouldn't it be fine if we could raise all our young to look at us and at our daughters and think of our design in terms of God's holy plan?

Marriage
And Spirituality

Mary Reed Newland

**Marriage is often conceived as the "lesser of two evils." It
ought not be so. The spiritual life for those of the married
state has its unique crosses and glories—but both must be
recognized and understood.**

I have a friend who is a career-girl, single and very attractive. Marriage, she says, is not her dish of tea. All of
which annoys most of her female friends, and they are forever trying to expose her to the right kind of man and what
they call her kind of marriage, ever hopeful that someday it
will take. "Jane," they say, "you just don't understand how
wonderful marriage can be. You haven't seen the right kind
of marriages—or you wouldn't be so hard to convince."

So it was no surprise to have them descend one day with
the announcement that "this is it"—they had the perfect
couple lined up, and all she had to do was meet them and
she'd be converted. She met them and marvelled at how
they were, indeed, perfect in every way—charming, devoted,
beautifully adjusted, living in the perfect apartment, he the
perfect provider and she the perfect homemaker and companion. It was too good to be true and for the first time

she was ready to concede that marriage didn't necessarily have to be more bickering than bliss.

Then several months later the man phoned with the shattering announcement that things were about to crack up. Would she come and talk to the light of his life? He had taken a severe beating in the market, their finances had done a right-about-face and suddenly, life was real, life was earnest. He was able to bear up under it, but apparently she wasn't, and what with having to give up a few pleasures and buckle down to a job, she was about ready to fly the coop. Jane was a working girl and happy in her job, maybe it would help if she'd give her a career-girl-type of pep talk. So Jane hiked over one night to listen to the whole tale of woe. This is how it went:

"My dear, you can't know what a mess it all is. I hate working, but I have to or we can't live the way we do, and Jack simply doesn't understand what its doing to me. Then to complicate things even more, his mother's been here for two weeks and I had to move all my clothes out and take a temporary apartment downstairs."

"Why the apartment downstairs? Don't tell me you can't put up with your mother-in-law for just two weeks?"

"My mother-in-law?" and the other woman screamed. "Oh darling! You don't understand—we aren't even married!"

A Holy Vocation

Marriage is a *spiritual union*. People can do all the things that are permitted in marriage outside of marriage—and there is no union. The whole thing hangs together because God says it does, and He feeds it a special kind of grace, grace reserved for the married alone, then He tells them what they are to be to one another, and He says that doing these things, they will give honor and glory to Him, for which reason He created them in the first place. He says the whole thing, from falling in love and making the decision to marry, to exchanging vows and giving each other freely in physical union, and to the ultimate end of the physical union, the bearing of children—all this, He says, is a holy vocation, a calling through which He calls us to Himself. This is how the married serve God—and it differs from any other vocation because it depends upon your loving and serving first of all one specific person, a husband or a wife, and secondly these specific children—and the love that is perfected in the service of these is the love we will know for all men.

But it's not easy, being married. It looks easy because we find our way to it through a series of shattering experiences with physical attraction (I do not mean sin—but just the discovery that we are capable of wanting to possess someone, and be possessed, in the full physical sense of the word) and because we know it first in the terms of physical love, we are apt to measure love forever after in these same terms. It isn't that at all. Physical love imitates God's love for the soul; when it is pure, it is good. After all, God invented it and all through Scripture His love for His Church is described in what some souls consider the most shocking physical language. All you have to do is read the Canticle of Canticles to come away with the conviction that God knows all about physical love and with the conviction that it's a pretty exalted thing. It's an exalted thing precisely because it is an imitation of an exalted thing—call it a facet of an exalted thing—but it is not the whole, nor will it last forever. Even in marriages that are unmarred by more than just ordinary every-day trials, it peters out, the passion is spent and the fires banked, and it becomes obvious that it has been only a means and not an end. It is a kind of *hors d'oeuvre*—a hint of things to come. It hints of a love that is waiting to be found but which, for lack of other words, must be described in the terms of physical desire.

We ought to know all this when we realize that physical love is easy—you literally "fall" into it. Those whose vocation is marriage do not have to sit down and talk to themselves into falling in love. It happens without any very apparent reason. And even for those who have not had the benefit of clinical texts on how to go about the specific act of nuptial love-making, instinct tells them what it is all about. Along with this, there goes with that first impassioned desire to possess and be possessed an equally impassioned desire to serve. Nothing is too much for the beloved, nothing too good. Nothing can be asked of us that we would not already want to give. All happiness is bound up in the happiness of the beloved and there is none outside of him. He is perfect—if not quite perfect, at least unique—and no one else is the combination of humor and wisdom and kindness and beauty as he. Foolish? Of course it is foolish, in a way. No one is that perfect. But that is how love makes people look perfect, and it's a very good thing, because one ought not go about getting married to merely a physique. These are the spiritual qualities we see, and this is the first step toward spiritual love. That is why it is all wrong to pooh-pooh physical love—it is an uncanny imitation of spiritual love and for some people (those called to marriage) it is the way to spiritual love.

So—we get married, and life is going to be beer and skittles ever after. Of course there's that little matter of "for better, for worse, for richer, for poorer, in sickness and in health," but who cares? To people who love each other as we do, nothing can make any difference. We are two minds with but a single thought—that we love each other. Whatever differences there are between us are the happy physical differences—they merely complement each other. Our marriage is going to be different from any other, we are going to be the exception. We both understand that we are called to be saints—we will be saints together. We have found a framework designed by God in which we can give ourselves to each other and still give ourselves to God. How easy!

What a sweet delirium—and God is kind to permit it. Because without the sweetness and the convictions, we would never have the courage to start. It is like the first abandon of a soul completely converted to a desire for nothing but God's will. I remember talking to a friend once and telling her that was how we had to love God's will—with abandon. And she said, hesitantly, "Yes—but I'm afraid. Afraid that if I do, He'll start doing a lot of hard things to me." That is like almost being in love, but not quite, because once you are—even if there is a small voice (or some small words: for better, worse, richer, poorer, sickness, health) you throw yourself into it with the conviction that love will make these things easy. And spiritual love does—that is where physical love is supposed to lead us. That is why it is no exaggeration at all to say that, for all its physical form, marriage is a spiritual life.

Growth in Holiness

Now spiritual growth depends on a lot of different things. It depends on prayer, vocal and mental, on meditation and contemplation, on attendance at Mass and the Sacraments, on spiritual reading, and particularly on a variety of forms of doing violence to one's self. And all these things are necessary to the development of anyone's spiritual life, no matter what his vocation. But the means to these things differ widely, and are governed by the mold of each vocation, and in no vocation, I am sure, is the spiritual life molded by things so much of the earth, earthy, as in marriage. The odor of sanctity, in marriage, is a distinct odor all its own—and only God could recognize it as such. To most ordinary noses it is a trying combination of burned toast and tobacco smoke and cooked cabbage and diaper pails, and a lot of other things too numerous and ridiculous to mention, with nothing whatsoever to indicate to the innocent bystander that these are the means to sanctification. Fasts and penances may be the way for the religious, and ministering to God's poor for the rich, preaching God's Word and reforming God's Sacraments for the clergy, but for the married, it is embracing what is there to be done within the four walls of their home.

MORTIFICATION

Take my good and noble husband, for instance, and the matter of mortification. Little did he, a man of delicate tastes and even more delicate digestion, realize that when he took unto himself a wife she would present him in no time at all with an array of children who, God be praised, would be fine and healthy and need their pants changed often. Nor would she rest there, but having decided to keep children, she must also decide to keep goats. However, never let it be said that the Lord is stingy with grace. My husband has met and conquered in the struggle with the concupiscence of the senses. His nose is at last mortified.

But it does not end there. Having become perfectly detached in the matter of what's in the breeze, this trial is exchanged for another which might be called "What's in a squeeze?" It all looked so providential at the time. The way the rider turned up, working the same shift, living on the same route—God shows His love in even the smallest things, we said, like figuring out a way to pay some of the expenses on the car. Ah yes—and whom the Lord loveth,

He chastiseth! So the providentially discovered rider turns out to be a man who sucks oranges! And into the furnace for Newland—this time it's his ears. Have you ever driven mile after mile in the dead of night sitting beside a man who squeezes and sucks oranges? "Darling," I said, "offer it up."

"Brother—don't think I don't!"

I have a pretty pamphlet in front of me now, with oodles of rules in it for the Christian married, and aside from the dogmas it repeats, the burden of success seems to rest on being clean and neat and dressing for dinner. Maybe we're screwy—but I can't say I have ever measured an upsurge of love for my mate at the sight of his freshly shaved chin. However I have sat in the kitchen at one-thirty in the morning waiting for him to get home from work, and I have loved him more, whiskers and dirty shirt and all, because for the sake of our children and myself, he has put up once more with forty-five minutes with an orange-sucker.

SILENCE

So much for mortification, only one of the ingredients of the spiritual life. Next, at random, take silence. Silence for the married would seem to be impossible. You've got to talk to each other. But it has its place—and that is in refusing to quarrel. One of the first disagreements to raise its head in our married life had to do with where to sit in church. My husband was brought up sitting in the middle. I was brought up sitting in the front. He, no matter how hard he tried, could not relax and pray in the front—he was overwhelmed by a sense of being on public display. I tried sitting in the middle and Mass became a kind of on-again-off-again peep show, which I attended while doing a ladylike buck-and-wing. I peeked to the left, I peered to the right, I saw the Ordinary through this lady's veil, and the Canon over that lady's feathers. It was exhausting, and

distracting, and completely unsatisfactory. I should add
that Bill is over six feet tall and hats are no distraction for
him. So sooner or later, I hate to admit it, we had words
over it. How could he persist in sitting in the middle when
I couldn't sit anywhere but in the front? And why didn't
he want to sit in the front? It was only a matter of getting
used to it—and if he loved God enough, surely he would
want to sit in the front. Now this last doesn't follow at all,
and it's a good thing all the people who do love God don't
want to sit in the front—there are only two front pews. But
no—he was adamant. He could not pray in the front. He had
a suggestion. Why didn't he continue to sit in the middle,
and I continue to sit in the front? I was horrified—this was
awful! We were *married,* we were supposed to be doing these
things *together.* It all indicated, to me, something terribly
wrong, and I plagued him unmercifully, with melancholy
sighs and broad hints and the wrong kind of silence every
Sunday after Mass. He, on the contrary, practised the right
kind of silence and never rose to the bait. And then, one
day, I overheard two women discussing us, with relish and
licking their chops. "...and you know what? They never sit
together at Mass! She sits in the front, and he sits in the
back. I wonder why???" And I howled, the whole thing was
too ridiculous and they'd never have believed the truth if
I'd told them. From the gleam in their eyes I could tell
they suspected all kinds of things—ultimately that we had
separate bedrooms, I'm sure. I'd given a good imitation of
a nagging wife and all for a difference in pews. Better to
have kept the peace and accepted his very good reasons
for sitting where he must, and waited for God to level the
mountains and fill the valleys of our life together. As He
has—in this regard. He has sent us a batch of children
who *have* to sit in the front—they're really too short to sit

in the middle. And mine spouse faithfully escorts them up there every Sunday morning. Me? Do I now enjoy Mass in a spirit of deep recollection? Not at all—I'm busy keeping track of my children.

PRAYER

Then there is the matter of prayer. Spirituality is dependent on prayer, so for the married, there must be much prayer. But one of the exasperating things about married life, after it is under way and the family begins to grow, is that there isn't too much time for prayer—at least not vocal prayer. So prayer, in the main, must be for the married mental prayer—that running conversation with God which is so easy but seems to be, for far too many, shrouded in mystery—if indeed they have heard of it at all. That is something I don't understand, and don't propose to waste time trying to figure out here. But I certainly think the news should be shouted from the housetops. Mental prayer is so simple it's absurd—"lifting the heart and the mind to God." It's really, I think, the easiest form of prayer, and its a natural for the married. In times of crises, whether they know it or not, people will use it instinctively. Like a mother who is frantic, looking for her child; "Please, God, please, don't let him be lost." Why wait till then to start having your own kind of conversation with God? You can do it all day long, whenever you're not having conversation with others. You find out after a while that it is so sweet that you'll begin to cut down on your conversations with others—unnecessary conversations. And when you can't employ mental prayer, you can employ whatever you are doing at the time as prayer. Contrarily enough, the more difficult a thing is to do, the more eloquent a prayer it makes. And it's surprising the number of things that will cease to be difficult once they have become prayer.

Penance

Then there is penance—another required subject in the pursuit of the spiritual life, and again, marriage is bursting with opportunities. In regard to penance, I am conducting a crusade—and to no avail at all—against hand lotions. All the propaganda put out by the makers and sellers of hand lotions makes me violently ill. Hand lotions will make or break the marriage, they shout. Ha! Hand lotions will make or break the makers of hand lotions—and no one else. Your husband will hate your raw red hands, they insist. Whose husband? Not mine. I don't hate the sight of his hands, up to and above his wrists, hanging out of the too-short sleeves of a jacket he's been wearing for years. Certainly it hurts his pride, but it serves as a very good penance. I don't think, when I see them, "How horrible—so ill fitting." They are more usefully occupied, even when they are just hanging limp, than a lot of hands in a lot of nicely tailored sleeves. And he doesn't think, when he sees my red hands in winter, "Disgusting—love is out the window." Of course if he did, I wouldn't do it—I'd even succumb to using the hand lotions, because one of the things a woman must do for her husband is try to look the way he wants her to look. But my husband happens to think that when Our Lady warned *Do Penance*—she meant penance. And if it's hand lotions versus penance, "then on you, honey, penance looks good." Before anyone gets the idea that I'm trying to paint a picture of us that is too-too noble, let me hasten to remind them that the idea isn't original with us. There is nothing so noble about penance. *Penance is due.* The whole idea originated with Jesus (and He was doing it for us). With Him it wasn't too short sleeves, or chapped skin, with Him it was nails.

POVERTY

And all this brings us to poverty. There are vocations within vocations, if that makes sense, and it is easy to see them in marriage. For instance, some families' vocation is poverty—and the wolf is hanging around the door on and off all their life long. With other families, it's sickness, and they have periodic brushes with death all their life long. For some, it's public scandal, and for others it's wealth—with the contingent obligation to provide for the poor. All of them lead souls to God, only along different paths. With us, up to now, it's been poverty; Holy Church makes us hopeful when she calls it "holy poverty."

It's not like the poverty of the religious—we took no special vow, except that "richer-poorer" part of the marriage vow. So I can't truthfully say that we embraced holy poverty. Rather, holy poverty embraced us. There was no doubt God wanted her to embrace us. At the time, you don't see too clearly why—except that it's His will and you pray for the grace to love it. Afterwards you can look back and see very clearly why—a lot of reasons why—but outstanding among them all is this: that it takes trial to teach you to love each other spiritually, trial to teach you to love God—and most of all, trial to teach you how God loves you. Isn't it a paradox?

One of the things that makes it difficult to adjust to poverty, even the idea of poverty, is that poverty is so embarrassing. This is not an age that sees Christ in the poor, and poverty never looks providential, just improvident. And the first step along the path is to do a general housecleaning in the matter of values; it helps to have the Gospels in hand. That was where our values had got themselves distorted. We had a fair-to-middling acquaintance with what Christ said in the Gospels, but having never been pushed to apply it much, it was so much pretty poetry. "Consider the lilies of the field" had never moved us to the point of ecstasy. But

when the screws begin to tighten, one is apt to go rushing
about looking for answers. We prayed like mad, and it had
no effect on the onrushing poverty. We tried to "help ourselves"—after all God helps those, *etc.* But to no avail. We
kept a stiff upper lip and a brave front before our family
and friends. All it seemed, from both inside and out, was
that we weren't smart enough, didn't know the right angles,
or if we did, hadn't tried them. Nothing ventured, nothing
gained, so we ventured the right angles. And poverty crept
closer and closer. And then one night, as usual searching
Scripture for the answers, a text we had read and heard
many times before jumped right off the printed page and
hit us between the eyes. "Your Father knows your needs
before you tell Him." Such relief, with that! Of course He
knew, so knowing we were growing shorter and shorter of
funds, and had so many needs, surely tomorrow He would
start to provide for them. But tomorrow, and tomorrow, and
tomorrow, He did *not* provide for them, and then the truth
began slowly to dawn. Maybe we had *other* needs, and they
were more important—and poverty was His way of providing
for them. It was a frightening prospect, awaiting God's good
time. We had no choice but to wait. He simply did nothing
about the poverty, at least nothing in the material sense.

But grace is always at work, and slowly the thing began
to taste sweet. If anyone had told either of us that waiting
hour by hour for the food to put in our children's mouths
would be sweet, we'd have assured them they were mad. But
that is what happens. He levelled us right to the ground by
refusing to bless our own efforts with success, and then He
showed us the bare palm of His hand by feeding us through
the efforts of others. People we have never even met, know
only by their names at the end of a letter, fed us in the
name of Christ. Humility is hard to come by, and when it

does you've got to be good to hang on to it. I hesitate to say we are humble because we have been poor—but at least now we know what humility is. For such stubborn flesh as we, it is not a lesson one learns by choice, but by force. We would have had to be incredibly blind not to see it. "Of yourself, you are nothing." Most people have to struggle to understand it and are at a loss to define it. But to the poor, God says, "Look, I'll show you." Nothing, nothing, nothing—everything we did came to nothing—but out of His love He provided for us through the love of others. Our families, our friends, and as I said, people we did not even know—but nothing came of our own efforts. And there was another aspect of humility held up to the light for us even baser, in the eyes of most people, than having to live on the alms of others: humiliation. To be thought a fool, a flop, a dead-beat. Brothers and sisters, that's hard to take! It's crammed down your throat until you choke on it, and then slowly you begin to develop the God's-eye-view. Especially the God's-eye-view of each other. Then you look past the familiar face and into the soul, and you understand what it means—to love spiritually. It's not the whole of it but all you can bear at the moment. "This Child is set for the fall, and for the resurrection...and for a sign which shall be *contradicted.*" How the Cross scandalizes the world! It's such a contradiction. It contradicts all the rules for success and happiness all the experts can cook up. Here, in contradiction, was love really beginning to bloom! Now it made the best sense it had ever made: "She is flesh of his flesh, and bone of his bone." If the married really want to understand what it means, then let them welcome the trials, nay—run to meet them. They come with commensurate grace, and grace over, and grace above, and grace until it spills over—and because grace is the gift of Love, if it is used, it begets love. We were no different from a thousand, a million, other couples who had been given a taste of poverty, or suffering, or whatever cross He chose to send, and we had thought all along that we loved each other. You don't begin to know what love is until you see your beloved suffer. Then, at last, you understand. *Marriage is a spiritual union.* Then you love not just with your heart, but with your soul.

IMMORTALITY

And there is one more (not one—a thousand, but this has to end somewhere!) ingredient in a recipe for spirituality for the married, and that is the children. They are the final proof, the incarnation, of the spiritual union. Let the physiologists wag their heads at such naiveté as this—and insist they are merely the result of a union in flesh. Pray for them because they do not know immortality when they see it. What a vocation marriage is! To be called to co-operate with Almighty God and have a part in His image and likeness. As St. Paul could write, "Christ is glorified in my body," so too can the married. In my body, and of my body, and through my body—and when the union of two brings forth one, and three, and five, and more is glorified again and again. Now understand the term "lay priests," who bring forth other Christs in a union so unreasonable that Coventry Patmore wrote of it that it is not unlike the Transubstantiation—wherein bread remains bread and wine remains wine, and the two become Christ. A man remains a man, and a woman a woman, and Christ says the "two become one flesh." We are so used to seeing children that we do not consider the miracle that they are. The whole thing is above reason. Marriage is a spiritual life which blossoms with immortality.

It occurs to me that perhaps this whole thing smacks of the too-good-to-be-true. Is there no dissonance anywhere?

Is this whole thing, for the Newlands, one long unending emotional and spiritual binge? No, it is not. But I do not intend to scandalize our public or our children by baring our feet of clay. It is enough to say we have them. Have we never awakened one not so fine morning and asked ourselves: "How did I get here?" Many times—and we've thrashed around and toyed with the idea that the whole thing was a big mistake in the first place. But—and this is my own private theory, it's possible I could be wrong—marriage is no mistake. Marriage *is*. It involves a gamble, a risk, and a good or a bad choice, but once a marriage is made, it's *the* way to God. He wants us—and He will have us, if only we will have Him. If I were to be limited to one rule on spirituality for the married, it would be to remember that no matter how tough it can be, how lonely at times, how unhappy, it can never be a solo flight—you've got to do it together.

"He Married an Angel"

Susan Candle

What happens when the wife of an average fellow gets religion? Mrs. Candle (a pen name) gives pointers on how to refrain from driving a husband to drink. Additionally there is some advice about some questions often overlooked by those who enter the married life without due preparation.

Now that so many things have been written and said about Christian marriage, and examples and patterns have been cited, and the Christian married who are moved to write about it have written about it, the burning question for a lot of the married—especially wives, who seem to worry about such burning questions—seems to be: "Fine, but what about my marriage? My marriage doesn't begin to measure up to these ideals. If being a saint depends, for the married, on the pursuit of the spiritual life *together,* planting gardens, joining study groups, reciting Compline, perfect and mutual abandonment to the will of God—then there's no hope for us. All we seem to share is roof, bed, board and our children, with struggles and problems thrown in, and very little else. Now and then we meet in a period of spiritual simpatico and I think we're off to a start, and then the whole thing collapses. What does it all mean? Is it my fault because I chose the wrong man? How could I have been so convinced he was right? Or was he right and now he's changed? Maybe I was too immature and now I've changed. Or did God play a trick on us? Did we choose with our hearts instead of our heads?"

And nowhere in any of the examples and patterns so many women search in hope of finding one for them, do they find one that fits. All look too good to be true, and, far from suspecting their authors of deliberate fabrication, the women who read them decide that whether or not one is permitted to be mediocre in the age of the lay apostolate, for such as themselves there is no choice. Mediocrity for the married seems to be inevitable for all but the chosen few, blessed apparently by some special grace at the time of choosing, smiled on by providence in the appearance of the right and perfect mate at the right and perfect time.

A word in defense of authors. The exuberance that goes with discovering the role of the married in the lay apostolate is such heady wine that for those married who write about it, the writing is apt to be heavily loaded on the side of the new joy discovered, the new concepts revealed, to the neglect of the all too familiar imperfections that still beset marriage. And for the Christian writer there is another difficulty in the form of discretion. Prudence puts great demands on the man or woman who, asked to write about Christian marriage, must choose between drawing it in big positive terms of his own and his mate's experience in spiritual growth, and sacrificing what inspirational message he may be able to pass along by the revelation of his own and his mate's human weaknesses in an effort to approximate reality. It's all very well for those who pay no compliment to the demands of charity to write "refreshingly frank exposes" of married life, for women to discuss their husbands' unfaithfulness or gambling or drinking, or for men to discuss their wives' preoccupation with clothes or money or birth control. But no Christian worth his salt can justify the betrayal of his spouse in any but the most innocuous and mildly amusing faults for publication for fear of running headlong into the serious sin of scandal. And the net result seems to be an inevitable distortion in even the most honest attempts to paint a picture of Christian marriage. People seeking patterns are eternal optimists and rarely read between the lines, and people trying sincerely to communicate big patterns almost always assume that what is left out will be read between the lines

No THING can do it

Spiritual growth for the married does not depend, and never did, on anything but the soul's hunger for God, and in that respect it differs in no way from spiritual growth in any other vocation. No house or garden or car, or lack of them, or homemade bread or Advent wreath or short breviary or any other *thing* can make a man a saint. And it's too bad if, in our enthusiasm for the right accessories, we give the impression that these things are going to make the big difference. They make a difference, but not *the* difference, and the preponderance of things written about the accessories seems too often to assume that of course everyone understands that the one big essential, still, is the holiness of the state. Unhappily, the impression far too many are left with is that plain marriage is not enough, and that unless things hew pretty well to the onward and upward direction for both partners at the same time all there is left is the best of a bad bargain. We have written about *ideals* and slightly overplayed our hand because we have given the impression that this is the whole of our experience. For the sake of

prudence we have omitted the things that fall short of the
ideal and given the impression they do not exist.

Women, because they are more concerned with expres-
sions of love, with emotion and atmosphere, fall into this
particular trap more easily than men. Until recently there
has not been too much clarification for women of what
women are made of. Maybe it's not sugar and spice and all
things nice, but it is as different from what men are made
of as sticks and snails and puppy-dogs' tails, and it would
help all women a lot to be able to see how different. Then
they can begin to see how vain is their sighing after "ever
two minds with but a single thought." The difficulty starts
because in the beginning two minds do have but a single
thought—mutually shared desire. It's after the desire has
ceased to predominate that the puzzling differences begin,
and develop in degrees from differences in tastes about
relatively unimportant things to wide gaps in interests and
pursuits and even, in many marriages, differences about
responsibility and duty and moral behavior. In some cases
it does go as far as moral behavior, as any priest hearing
confessions well knows. That this is so even in marriages
between two fairly enlightened Christians proves that knowing what is right is still no guarantee of doing what is right.
The fact that a man is a member of the Mystical Body is
no deterrent to the Devil.

WIVES ACQUIRING SPIRITUALITY
It must give the Devil particular delight to muddy up
the issues in a marriage—especially if one of the issues is
the newly awakened spiritual growth of the woman. Maybe
one of the reasons they are easily muddled on this score is
that so much of the material dealing with spiritual growth
has been presented from the feminine point of view, with
emphasis on virtues which come easy (or anyway easier,

because the capacity for them has been built in) for women: self-sacrifice, service, devotion, love, compassion and so on. The mistake many wives make is to respond to the call to a deeper spiritual life through these channels and expect their husbands to do likewise. They grow a bit in abandonment, develop a taste for frugal poverty, and are upset because their husbands are still concerned over security. They do not stop to reflect that it is the nature of a man to be protector and provider; the drive to provide security is part of his very being.

Physical love they give willingly out of their new understanding of its sacramental beauty, and they are shattered to find that often the desire they respond to seems nothing more than hunger to be satisfied, with little of the mystical quality that is part of a woman's giving of her love. Even the bearing of children, so mysterious and satisfying an experience for a body designed to carry them and a heart quick to expand and savor every day and week of even the most trying pregnancy, can become a matter of serious discord. To the prospective fourth- or fifth- or sixth-time father worried over finances, the approaching child sometimes seems to mean more in terms of added expense and increased responsibility than dazzling immortality. "I've got four wonderful kids I wouldn't take a million for, but I wouldn't give a nickel for another."

The wives are drawn to a more active participation in liturgical life, daily Mass, daily Communion, and are horrified to see that their husbands can take just so much of it and, past that point, prefer to leave it alone. "You live your spiritual life and let me live mine." All these things and more stab at women who want nothing more than to grow in God and find new and keener happiness for their husbands by sharing the growth. They try to communicate what they have learned, and when it meets with little or no response they are lost and hurt and resign themselves to making the best of a sorry marriage, an innocent mismating, and going the rest of the journey spiritually alone.

MEN HAVE A DIFFERENT WAY

Perhaps there are marriages where none of these things have been problems. Perhaps there are couples who have walked the whole way hand in hand with never a cross word between them—if so, they are rare. The married saints are still not common, and it would take the wisdom and holiness of a pair of saints to meet with perfect understanding every one of the clashes inevitable between two creatures created so different in their natures.

Women err—often innocently—in their desire for perfection in themselves and their husbands by expecting that the *way* will be identical. Circumscribed by the walls of their homes, intensely occupied with their duties as wives and mothers, they are often unable to project themselves to the totally different problems of their husbands, who go off every day into a world they no longer know. It is a happy complement, the contrast in the nature of the sexes—the man busy providing, planning, protecting, the woman creating harmony in the home he provides, bearing and raising the children, listening, sympathizing, encouraging. The combining of two such natures in one sacrament makes, indeed, another one—more complete and perfect for this vocation than a combination of two planners, providers, protectors or two harmonizers, listeners, sympathizers. And because this is so, it follows that the framework of the vocation does describe a way for the two of them which is identical—but which still subdivides to be different on the intimate level of their male and female natures.

A crude example of the difference can be seen in house-hunting. They are both interested in finding the same thing—the right house—but when they look at a house together, he goes down into the cellar to inspect the pipes, the heating plant, the foundation, while she is busy deciding which bedroom would be right for whom, where she will put her furniture and whether the house as a whole fits the life she dreams of making for her family. If he calls her downstairs to look at the furnace, she looks and says, "If you say its good, dear, then that's fine with me—I don't know a thing about furnaces—but I do wish you'd come up and see the bay in the dining room. My curtains will be perfect there, and for plants it's ideal." The difference in the way each looks at the house is no mystery and causes no arguments because it is a matter of tangibles. The same difference holds in regard to their approach to the spiritual life—but it's harder to understand because here they are dealing with intangibles.

Many women, when they understand this better, must admit honestly that in their drive for sameness in their own and their husbands' approach to the spiritual life, they have often done more damage than good to the spiritual advancement of the very ones they love best. Witness the classic retort to a pastor who asked a husband if he realized his wife was practically a saint. "Yes, I suppose so—but do we have to have religion for breakfast, lunch *and* dinner?"

No Sense of Humor

In marriages where this sort of thing is a problem, the typical spiritually-hungry wife reads avidly all she can get her hands on, rejoices in her discovery of a new world of spiritual values and sets out enthusiastically to transform herself and her husband. Unable to see that the very sound of the words "the little way" might leave him cold, her enthusiasm to communicate what she has discovered is soon dampened. She ceases the attempt to reveal such a way to him but at the same time is unable to cease measuring him by it. Picking up a pin for the love of God may be sheer joy and sweetness to her, but she fails to see that her husband possibly does not even see pins and if he does, can't get very excited about picking them up.

Why blindness to her own faults sets in at this time it is hard to say, but that is usually what happens. She becomes acutely aware of how inadequate she is in the eyes of God, yet is increasingly baffled at how her husband can find anything lacking in her. She tries harder than ever to please him—he might at least show some appreciation instead of accepting it as his due. She demands fewer things, sighs less after the world—perhaps somewhat audibly, with explanations of why she sighs less—and he begins to wear the strained look of a man who has just discovered his wife should have been a nun. The more her hunger for God grows, the more he seems to wish she would hunger after Him less and substitute instead the return of her sense of humor. And if she points out that she has not lost her sense of humor, that it is merely elevated and no longer so earthy, he is apt to grunt that he liked it earthy, and if this new elevation is humor—then it ain't funny. If her prayer life increases, her devotions, spiritual reading, visits to church, she definitely observes that he, if busy at all, is busy only at paring his down. Their home becomes increasingly a "little temple of God" to her but he seems drawn to spend more time away from it. And in her hurt and bewilderment the best she can come up with is to "offer it up."

A NICE DODGE

Do not misunderstand. This is not meant to belittle "offering up." But in a very real way, for people with hurt feelings, offering up is a nice dodge for avoiding self-examination. There are some things we are better off hugging to ourselves. Especially for women pursuing perfection at full gallop, indiscriminate offering up often leads farther and farther off center. There are cruelties and injustices which can be borne no other way (also such things as celery crunching, knuckle cracking, and toast crumbs in the butter), but real spiritual growth is not forthcoming without real self-examination. In proportion to her effort to know herself, to see the puniness of her own reflection cast against the mirror of Christ, many a woman has learned to laugh at her fancied miseries, to see herself far more accurately as having dished out the same kind of misunderstanding according to a different rule of thumb.

For instance, for women who don't drink, married to men who do but are still not qualified alcoholics, the art of keeping hands and sharp tongues off is painfully learned. And for women who don't drink and are trying their wings at the art of self-denial, the Devil loves to spotlight brightest of all the areas of their husbands' over-indulgence, being careful to relegate to a place well down-stage their own addiction, say, to cigarettes or long telephone conversations. The incipient danger in the former may outweigh that in the latter, but in terms of time stolen from marital duty, the shirts she doesn't get ironed or the dishes she doesn't wash, all because of a mid-morning break with a cigarette in one hand and the telephone in the other (for all they may be discussing the latest in liturgical living), are as much neglect as the hour he wastes having a quick one with the boys from the office instead of coming home to fix the leak under the kitchen sink. And should he take profane exception one morning to the fact that the buttons are still off his shirt and might not be if she'd cut out most of her gabbing, she is quick to remind him she has not stirred outside her domain for days, is completely devoted to her duty as he well knows and doesn't see how he can criticize her telephoning when he wastes just as much time hanging over bars. Her husband might well reflect (and probably does) that since she is the one who is determined to be a saint, her breach of obedience to duty is relatively far graver than his—who claims to be no more than a nice ordinary slob. And he probably takes two hours for a quick one the next time.

Much as women hate to admit it, if they are really serious about their desire for sanctification, this sort of thing does apply. No man who has not caught the flame is going to be moved one iota closer to the goal by his wife's continually pointing out how far he is away from it. At this point the well-worn joke applies: "What is the definition of a martyr?" "A martyr is someone who is married to a saint." There are more men than you can shake a stick at who go around indulging their weaknesses all because their wives have discovered the spiritual life and are bent on reforming them. For some it is no more than resistance in commonplace ways—a diminishing of courtesy, an increase of profanity, an over-assertion of masterfulness in their treatment of their children. For some it may be more serious. But underneath it all is the determined effort not to be swallowed up by what is fast becoming a smothering display of virtue.

That sanctity does not consist of *displays* of virtue was pretty well proved by the nuns murmuring outside St. Therese's door as she lay dying: "What will Reverend Mother ever write about Sister Therese—she has really done nothing." Getting lost in exaggerations of virtues, in the minor details of perfection, and losing sight of the biggest issue of all—that holiness is learning to love to the highest degree—trips so many women up.

Aggrieved Silence

But there are real hardships as well as fancied ones in marriage, and the spiritual approach is certainly the only way to bear them. The only trouble is that it's not half as easy as it looks. For instance, it is a real discovery to begin to understand the value of silence. But silence in the hands of an aggrieved woman (even justifiably aggrieved) is as much an irritant as her former haranguing. And the husband who is well aware that some neglect or abuse of his is painful to his wife is rarely moved to examine himself contritely by the sight of her woebegone face, surrounded by the deep well of her silence. His reaction is more apt to be, "Dammit, if nobody's going to speak to me at home, I'll go where they will."

Silence is better than quarrels (at least after all possible prudent attempts to settle a disagreement have been tried and failed). But we are supposed to use silence so that God can speak to us. Used this way (minus self-pity), even the most cruel domestic thorns have a way of slowly diminishing as the reality of eternity and God's love begins to take their place.

One woman married to a man whose extreme sense of insecurity moved him to lash out constantly in intolerable displays of temper and criticism, learned the only way to keep her silence from becoming mere wound-licking was to think of something she could do that would please him—a meal she could cook, a pair of slacks she could press, or merely the resolve to sit and watch TV with him all night if he wanted it, although she heartily despised everything he liked. She learned to wrench her mind away from the sting of his injustices and busy it planning an act of love (dry as cinder, but a purer act of love for its dryness) that would help fill up what was wanting at the moment in their union.

They Belong Together

Of course that is the clue—the oneness of the union. When one member suffers, so does the other—whether the suffering is the kind that is shared, like sickness, shock or loss, or inflicted. The woman who has really terrible pain to suffer in her marriage must keep reminding herself that her own pain is part of the cross which she must bear, in one form or another, if she is serious about wanting to be a saint—while the sickness of soul that afflicts her mate is the really great tragedy. The salvation of an imperfect marriage lies in an awareness of the obligation to fill up what is wanting in the weakness of each other. It is the peculiarity of the vocation that neither man nor woman is any longer "whole" alone. "My better half" is no catch phrase for the married, but an accurate description of the spouse one is bound to love better than oneself. Their marriage is a common vessel into which they have poured themselves and there is no longer any way to God but in it.

Understanding this, unhappy women can begin to see the childishness and folly of such indulgences as day-dreaming over husbands that might have been, and also avoid the subtly hidden but dangerous traps to which such indulgences lead. One woman, rueing aloud in the presence of her children her choice of the wrong man instead of the right, so soured the whole concept of marriage for her daughters that she robbed them of even a fair share of optimism when it came their turn to pick mates.

Idle designs for "getting even" are the same kind of folly and grow directly out of the refusal to meet weakness with understanding, injury with forgiveness and love. "If he won't do this then I'll be darned if I'll do that." One woman who responded to her husband's refusal to accept family responsibility decided to repay in kind by indulging in harmless flirtations. She ended up committing the far

worse sin of infidelity, with the final step the divorce court
and their two children living with a grandmother.

Succumbing to temptations against loyalty, temptations
to seek too frequent balm for wounds by betraying a husband's imperfections to family and friends, not only does
not right what is wrong but in the end eats away at the
weakened fabric of what love is left. Gradually, from marriage to a man with whom she knows somehow she must
reunite herself, hers becomes a marriage to a man whom she
feels somehow she must endure.

Some relief from serious tensions is necessary and can
be found in the outpouring of woes—but not profitably
unless the confidante she chooses is able to help her see
things objectively, and has faith that the graces of the vocation will not be found wanting. A confessor or an older
woman wise in the ups and downs of marriage can do much
to help, whereas a next-door neighbor quick to sympathize
and agree that she does, indeed, have a hard row to hoe can
do terrible damage.

The woman who has been given the grace of a greater
hunger after holiness can use her spiritual growth creatively.
She can cover her husband's weakness rather than expose it,
delineating his virtues for their children, shielding his faults
from family and friends. She can build on what is good and
sound, and add, out of her growing love for Christ, new love
for him—shored up by prayers for the grace to love when
loving grows difficult. Secure in the knowledge that God
sends grace in abundance to each according to his need and
that, after she has done all she knows how, the cure for their
ills is in His hands, she can gradually learn to relax and let
God in His own time work all things to good.

It may take the whole of her life, but long before it is
over she will understand that the times of unbearable pain

have been the most fruitful. The burning away of self in pain, the emptying of her own will, purifies her love of self-interest, and she can begin to see the enormity of Christ's love for her own soul and the soul of her husband. No longer is her marriage like a chance mismating, nor the frictions the result of ill-chosen partners drawn together and imprisoned in a union that has far too little *better* in it, and far worse than *worse*. And looking back over the trials which have been the hardest to bear, she will discover that they seemed to be especially designed for her. To a woman who cherishes solvency, the yoke of debts and mismanagement of family money is a cross of almost unendurable weight. To the woman who delights in respect of persons, the public displays of a drinking husband before the eyes of family and friends are almost impossible to bear. To the woman who likes to reason, analyze, "talk things out," marriage to a man who deliberately blinds himself to reason and defies all rules of fairness to assert his authority is a torment.

Facing up to One's Own Faults

It is when she begins to understand that part of her suffering has been the result of her own pride, that she can begin to recognize other areas of imbalance where her own distortions have been to blame. For instance, the woman who makes a fetish of housekeeping, who goes overboard in the pursuit of *order,* may find that in her passion for everything in its right place and the creation of a "tranquil atmosphere" in her home, she has been lacking in warmth and companionship. On the other hand the woman who is too offhand about trying to keep things in order, who airily ignores the call to conventional housewifeliness for the pursuit of intellectual improvement, may find that the clue to her husband's chronic irritability lies in the eternal stack of unwashed dishes.

Even the woman who, on fire with charity, sees Christ in her neighbor and rushes to tend her neighbor's every need, step into the breach, care for the children, take her neighbor's children in—may find that in her enthusiasm to serve Christ in all men she has come perilously close to spreading herself too thin, taking on more than she can handle, and in a very real way displeasing—perhaps even disobeying—the wishes of her husband and letting the needs of her own children go begging. (This may sound like treason, but it is a common form of apostolic greediness among women of good will not only to want to serve all men, but to *try* to—and leave nothing for the *other* Christs to do.)

In marriages where spiritual discord exists, these errors committed in the best faith can well aggravate the situation. The spiritual growth of a wife must help her eventually to accept her share of the guilt, bend every energy to correct it, and if there are still differences to understand that if she loves as she should they should *make* no difference. For lack of demonstrations of affection, she must abide quietly in the conviction that she is loved, even if it does not show too often. (This is not self-delusion—with rare exceptions, if there was love once, it is still there. Sometimes it takes near-tragedy to bring it to light, but it is there.) For lack of understanding, she must contribute understanding. For lack of increased spiritual activity, she must keep hands off and pray for an increase of spiritual activity.

There are still other marriages with trials which seem to be permitted not so much as instruments of filling in the valleys and levelling the mountains of faults, but as mysterious invitations to plumb the frustration of Christ's love as He suffered alone in the Garden, and draw closer to Him in a union of pain. There are women who want many children and are married to men who don't—and won't. There are women who are radiantly pure and faithful, married to men who aren't. And there is that common and tragic suffering of women who are married to alcoholics. It's no use blinking such situations as these when writing of Christian marriage, dismissing them loftily with a few obvious phrases about the imprudent choice of mates, the lack of mature preparation or ignorance of Christian duty and the marriage ideal. These things exist—yet they are still not impediments to sanctity. Where they exist—they are the means to it. And where they exist and there are women who must admit they exist, articles describing how things "should be" are no help at all. No one knows better than such wives how things should be. They want to know what to do with things the way they are.

This article would be unbearably presumptuous if it pretended to be the answer. Nor does it pretend that no one has tried yet to give any answers. Call it an appeal in behalf of the greater number of the married (in particular the wives—let someone else write about the husbands) whose marriages are far from living up to the patterns so far exhibited. What they want to be told, in a better way than this writer can tell them, is that whether their trials are small, medium or large, they are the stuff of which sanctity is made. Their vocation by its very commonness hides heroism more successfully than any other vocation. It has none of the romantic allure of the vocation of the contemplative religious. It has none of the derring-do of the missionary vocation in foreign lands. Because it is the vocation of the multitude, far too few remember to tell them it is the one vocation that peoples the world. Nuns and priests, bishops and popes are born of marriages, and statesmen and geniuses and prophets—and saints. Out of all kinds of marriages—

not just the happy ones—come the people whom Christ has bade carry on the work of the redemption.

And the women and men who must face the fact that terrible differences divide them in their marriages must also know that the path of the differences itself can be productive. Pain is fruitful, and purifies—the whole scheme of the redemption revolves around One Man's pain. And where there is one who is good and longs to be holy, married to one who is not and does not, then thank God that in marriage they are one, because by the love and prayer and sacrifice and pain of the whole member the afflicted member may be saved.

Once there was a girl who prayed and prayed for the grace to choose the right husband, but still she was not sure. And she went for the umpteenth time to her confessor and said: "I've prayed and prayed, and still I'm not sure. I want so badly to do God's will—to be a saint, but supposing my choice is a mistake?" And he said the funniest thing. He said: "Suppose it is—what of it?"

POVERTY AND MARRIAGE

Ed Willock

"Poverty"—that word no one likes to hear. Surely it doesn't apply to those who are married. "Such a state is only for religious!" Of course, there is a difference—but what kind? And how?

St. Francis of Assisi would have acted differently had he been married. You can bet on that. After the "I do's" have been uttered and the golden handcuffs dropped smoothly but firmly on the wrists, any call from the spirit must be answered in writing and endorsed with two signatures. Delightful though it may be, and truly a road to sanctity, matrimony is still a wing-clipping ceremony. Whether a spouse wishes to retire to a local bar for a beer, or a local church for a prayer, due regard must be given to the ties that bind.

This is one side of the story, and the side you are most likely to hear repeated. If this were the complete story we might conclude that, as far as the married are concerned St. Francis was just a holy crack-pot, and we may retire to our beauty rests undisturbed by any qualms of conscience as to the obligation of holy poverty. Things are not quite as simple as that.

Marriage is not, as so many couples suppose, a brace of tickets for front seats in the amphitheater from which we may watch the religious and the celibates being thrown to the lions. The road to Calvary is just as rough whether we traverse it single file or in couples. It is still a road of sacrifice. Over and above the fact of the difficulties that line the primrose path there is still the business of voluntary poverty, a self-inflicted detachment from the pottage of life, and it is meant for all Christians whether married or not. St. Francis would have acted differently had he been married, but this does not mean that he would have divorced Lady Poverty. It means that he would have embraced her in a different way. He would have resolved the paradox of voluntary detachment in the midst of necessary attachment, for this is the special problem of the Christian married.

The Call to Poverty

Catholics in ever-increasing numbers are coming to realize that the Faith in our times is being asphyxiated by an insidious gas called the bourgeois spirit. This spirit is the impetus behind the mystical pilgrimage to the shrine of Mammon frequently referred to as "getting ahead." It is the identification of human happiness with the ever-increasing accumulation of stuff. Even the pagans are becoming sick of it. Holy poverty is the one round peg that fits the nasty hole of our vacuous concupiscence.

Many married people have heard this story and like it. They find it hard, however, to relate voluntary poverty to the growing demand for goods that goes with raising a family. The rat race of bargain hunting, overtime work, renewal of furniture, paying the rent, procuring dishes and diapers, dresses and drain-pipes...this is a crucifixion they would gladly escape. The sigh goes up, "If we could only afford to be poor! How nice it would be not to *need* all these things." I have talked the whole business over with people so bothered, and I should like to attempt a kind of ground-plan for marital poverty. It will be brief and incomplete, but it should do something more than scratch the surface.

POVERTY AND ADMINISTRATION

I think the key to the problem is found in a contrast between the poverty of St. Francis and the poverty of La Trappe. The poverty of Francis was sudden, spontaneous, complete, and uncalculated. The poverty of the Cistercians is quiet, ordered, partial, and calculated. Both forms of poverty are rigorous enough so that no one can accuse me of watering down. In both cases, poverty is a means to the end of holiness. Yet they differ in practice. Why the difference?

Naked poverty must remain the privilege of those who have no temporal institution to maintain. When Francis stripped himself naked before his Bishop, and ran through the forest singing, he stripped only himself, and he ran alone. He had nothing to lose, and his deprivation deprived no one but himself. On the other hand, once an institution is founded, whether it be a monastery or a family, an order must be devised to sustain it and maintain it. Poverty can only be a means to this end. The rule and the order is the whole, of which poverty is a part. If poverty were to be forgotten in either institution, it would be better that the institution collapse. If poverty became primary, then the institution would collapse. A program of complete poverty can only be pursued at the sacrifice of institutions.

The family must be maintained as an institution, so poverty in marriage should be ordered, partial, and calculated. This does not necessarily limit the fervor of those who seek God, it merely limits the sphere in which the fervor is exercised. A father can still give his heart and mind to God and yet continue to administer property. A mother can give

herself to God but it will be manifested mainly in the service
of her husband and children. It's pretty obvious that the home
cannot be run as though it were a Trappist monastery. We
cannot cut the children, down to a minimum diet nor get
them out of bed at 2:30 A.M. for Matins and Lauds. Singing the Office in choir would have its drawbacks. Without
getting too involved in distinctions, the family is inclined
to operate on the active principle rather than the contemplative and would consequently have a discipline unlike that
of La Trappe. For the purposes of defining holy poverty for
families, I have taken the liberty of dividing the discipline
into four categories. Poverty in the family is specific. It is
ingenious. It is communal. It is, above all, patient.

MARITAL POVERTY IS SPECIFIC

Matrimony is specific. "Do you take *this* woman? I take
thee John. *This* is my wife. *This* is my home. *These* are my
jewels." The choice is emphatic and discriminating. Both nature and grace impose upon the married a specific obligation
for specific persons. Since the family exists not only to bear
but to raise children, then the parent is obliged to produce
and to maintain specific things, *the things that the specific
persons need.* The fact that matrimony is specific does not
mean that love and affection *terminates* in any one creature
or is confined to any four walls, for that is idolatry. What
it does mean is that marital love is centripetal, generating
outward from a specific love affair, a love affair in which
Christ Himself is a partner and the first principle.

Holy poverty in marriage, then, is detachment from
all things except those *specific* things that are required to
maintain *this* family in the frugal comfort that encourages
virtue. The revolutionary implications of this definition may
not be immediately obvious. If you just think for a moment
about all the things that the advertisers say we *all* need, and

then think of how many of these things that most of us *do not need at all,* then you get a glimmer. Rooms in which small children play *do not need* shiny waxed floors. Every family *does not need* a car. Every child *should not* go to college. Every child *should not* get a new Easter outfit. Every home *should not* have a washing machine. Every child *should not* have his own bedroom. Without exaggeration, a million such statements could be made. One man's meat is another man's poison. One family's needs are another family's rubbish. Holy poverty rids itself of all impedimenta whether in fact or in desire.

Most families that I know who are trying to practice holy poverty have to a great degree solved the problem of luxuries. They haven't any. This happy state is usually achieved by accepting the beggars that God sends whether by way of the door or by way of the womb. Self-denial then becomes a question of denying one legitimate need so as to provide another. For example...

A mother badly needs dental work. Frequent toothaches are making her irritable with the children. The car which Father needs at work is about ready to yield up the ghost for lack of a new clutch. It is possible to afford one, but not both. There's the problem. Whatever the decision, self-denial is involved. If Daddy gets his clutch, he feels like a heel. If Mother has her teeth fixed, she worries about Daddy all day long. St. John of the Cross could find but little pleasure in such an indulgence.

A father is an ink renderer working for an inadequate salary. If he could take a course in drafting, he would make more money. He saves from his lunch money. Just as he has acquired enough for the course, Muriel, age six, gets bad tonsils. The doctor says they must come out. Daddy remains an ink renderer for another three years.

Father needs a new tool. Mother needs a new coat. The children need new shoes. The children get the shoes. Father gets a headache. Mother gets the once-over at Sunday Mass.

I have made no reference here to families who have more than they need, or to those whose needs are always adequately cared for. Such families, to practice poverty, must go outside the family circle. In most cases justice, not charity, demands this. It isn't hard to find someone who needs what you have in abundance. You usually sit beside such a person at Sunday Mass.

Poverty is Ingenious

We can presuppose that a Christian family grows normally in children planned *for* and not *against*. Few enterprises receive less encouragement. Not even the founding of a religious foundation goes so unapplauded or unaided by a secular world as does the maintenance of a large working-class family. Since this is the case, the poverty of such a family must be ingenious. In every way the parents must try to provide by their own labors the necessities they cannot afford at the stores. The things they must buy requires a mastery of the art of bargain-hunting to pay as little as possible for the best quality.

A few yards of muslin and some boxes of dye provide cheerful draperies for the living-room windows. A bit of skill with tools and a trip to the distributors replaces a cracked hinge on the refrigerator at a small fraction of the cost of having it serviced. A set of second-hand clippers prevents a clipping at the hands of the local barber every time the kids become shaggy.

A few extra dollars spent at the right time for vegetables in quantity, to store or can, means a saving over a period of months. A cobbler's last comes in handy. A woman needs a good sewing machine. Practical nursing and an eye for symptoms keeps the doctor away except in serious cases.

What, you may ask, has all this got to do with poverty? Tools and skills are, in fact, riches, perhaps the only kind of material riches. Then why call it poverty? The poverty lies in the denial of luxuries, pleasures, rest, and comfort that must be made in order to purchase the tools and use them. You can't sit down and listen to "Inner Sanctum Mysteries" while there are two chairs to be mended. It is something to forego the ingratiating courtesies of the "Nice Store" clerks in order to crawl with the rest of the proletariat through mounds of goods on the bargain counter. You continue to wear the same shabby suit so that you can afford some plumbing tools. You work at the sewing machine until well after midnight when there are no tiny hands to get at the thread. For her birthday Mother gets a new pump for the antiquated washer. For his birthday Daddy gets a brace and bit so that he can re-assemble the kitchen furniture. The price of *Theology and Sanity* is expended on yard-goods for junior's coat. The cost of a night-out is represented in the new paint-job on the old crib for the new baby. This is ingenious poverty.

MARITAL POVERTY IS COMMUNAL

This point requires much more consideration than I can give it here. We have been acting on the fallacy that families exist in a vacuum. We have forgotten that a family must be part of a community of families. Being poor as a church mouse is tough on church mice because mice do not practice mutual charity. In the usual run of things deprivation and prosperity alternate in our lives. In a community it is seldom likely that everyone will be impoverished or, at least, be without the same things at the same time. This fluctuation in affluence is the natural occasion for neighborliness. "What have I got that you need, what have you got that I need?"

We must rebuild communities within and without the cities by reviving the economic system of mutual charity. This is already being done in many places. The breakdown of our present economy (an economy that cannot provide homes or decent food *is* broken down) is having the providential effect of throwing people together in mutual cooperation. Since every family, especially the father, should be engaged in restoring the community, holy poverty in our times must be communal.

All those who are convinced of the need for inter-family cooperation, will, as soon as they act upon it, discover that they must deny themselves certain pleasures, wealth, and comforts so that they can work with others to build homes, organize cooperatives, sponsor parochial units, found maternity guilds, operate family services, attend retreats and study meetings, aid the stricken, shoulder the burdens of the fallen...and so on, endlessly, practicing denial *as a family* so that the institution of the family will be preserved.

MARITAL POVERTY IS PATIENT

It would seem that the very wolves that snap at the flanks of the family are those extremely useful crosses that must go with family life. The constant demands for food, clothing and shelter, the bearing with sickness, weakness, and death, are the scourging disciplines that make the parent lean and trim to run so as to win. The firm demands of circumstance serve the same purpose in the married state as the rigorous rule provides for the monastic.

Though the poverty (as I have defined it) must be measured and planned, there is no way of avoiding the unforeseen crosses to which the family in particular is prey. It stands to reason, then, that all voluntary deprivations serve their best purpose, not in merely cleaning the decks for action, but in disciplining the will to do the Will of God. If we deny ourselves the things we could have (the night-out for the new crib) then it will be easier for us to accept graciously the trials we cannot avoid. Voluntary poverty must be patient or else it will be no more than stoicism or human competence. The plan will become everything. We will become poverty snobs. In the name of thrift we will become misers. We will be as proud of what we do as the bourgeois are about what they *have*.

Austerity is not virtue. It is merely the soil in which virtue will grow if grace plants the seed, and Christ brings it to fruition.

ONE AND ONE IS ONE

Ed Willock

Marital fidelity is becoming scarce. Beside this fact all other symptoms of social disintegration are comparatively insignificant. Infidelity has been caused primarily by the ostracism of Mary from modern life. Without her, feminine modesty is ignored; men divide women into good and bad, and treat them accordingly. The specific for the social disease of infidelity is a restoration of dignity to women in public life by reference to Mary the Virgin, and in private life by reference to Mary the Mother.

APART AT THE SEAMS

Statistics and Kinsey Reports are not the most effective means of finding out prevailing opinions and customs concerning the impermanence of wedlock. Sexual inquisitions are not likely to evoke testimonies more intelligible than a blushing whimper or a boastful simper. No sampling of opinions is valid that limits the inquiry to those who not only are lascivious but are willing to brag about it.

I have heard tell of only one instance in which such a consultation resulted in a normal reaction on the part of the *client*. It was a first-hand report of a young man who did his part in World War II acting as secretary to various psychiatrists who interviewed reluctant recruits for the Navy.

Those libido-explorers felt obliged to ask intimate questions to determine (each according to his own standard) whether the recruit was over or under-sexed. On the particular day in question the interviewee was a young red-head, newly married, who approached the encounter with a convinced belligerence.

In his best couch-side manner the psychiatrist asked his first routine question, "How do you get along with your wife?" My secretary-friend gleefully reported that the young man answered, "None of your damn business," and planted an ample fist in the beaming countenance of his inquisitor. Seldom does a psychiatric consultant establish so rapid and effective a contact with his client. The result contributes very little to science of course, and does not provide our healthily inquisitive minds with more data on boudoir mores among moderns.

Pertinent judgments fortunately do not depend inevitably upon the scientific method of investigation. Common sense and intuitive perception have always served men well and have not as yet been invalidated by Hooper or Gallup. The value of Kinsey Reports is limited. Royalties accrue to their authors; they objectify lust and thus, according to the modern mind, make it respectable (everybody does it!) and, much like Christian apologetics, serve more to confirm already established convictions than to enlighten ignorance.

We have no need to snoop into intimate places to learn that marital fidelity is somewhat less popular than baseball. Anyone who has spent some fraction of his life in offices, shops, clubs, poolrooms, barracks or movie theaters, *knows* with justifiable assurance that husbands chase after strange women and wives chaff under the restriction of one husband. Precisely how many couples remain faithful to one another out of convention, conviction or convenience may be a mystery, but everyone knows that *religious* fidelity is the quiet, unphrased conviction of but a minority. The most convincing evidence that marital fidelity is disappearing is the disappearance of all those customs, habits and opinions without which fidelity is unlikely. Tandem polygamy is socially permissible. Monogamy is looked upon not as a virtue but as a feat of endurance. The unattached female is the idolized symbol of American womanhood. Even those who are faithful to their spouses connive via the movies with the evil liberty of flitting from flower to flower. Young people have abandoned the bastion of pre-marital celibacy and have raised their flags over fidelity to one *date* during a given period of time that becomes ever shorter. These customs testify more damningly than Kinsey.

THE COMMON FAMILY

Infidelity is a mortal sin. That means you go to Hell if you do it. Infidelity is a betrayal of God and of your spouse, and of humanity. These are the best reasons for avoiding it. If I refer here to other evils which flow from infidelity and provide other reasons for fearing it, I do so not because I feel that the argument of damnation and betrayal is no longer valid, but because I feel that too many Catholics who never question the need for fidelity in their own lives, pass off the fact of infidelity among their neighbors as a thing of small concern. Secularism has marked us to the degree that we regard as optional for others the moral sanctions which for us are obligatory. We cling to our own salvations and the integrity of our own families without compassion for the lives and families of others.

We are so calloused because we no longer regard life and possible salvation as a thing which we possess in *common* with all mankind. Our family is but one cell in the fam-ily of mankind and in the Mystical Body of Christ. If one part of the Body is diseased the whole will suffer. Marital infidelity is a social disease tremendously contagious, that morally threatens the life of society and cripples the efficacy of the Mystical Body.

When the family, which is the basic social unit, disintegrates, then society is not only sick, but it has lost the principle of its own recovery. Cracks in the wall of a building are not half as serious as the fact that the mortar which binds the bricks is turning to sand. Enmities between classes and cliques, races and creeds, are not so dangerous as the prevalent enmity between husbands and wives. All social contracts depend for their strength upon the strength of the marriage contract.

It is in the home that the child receives his instructions in loyalty. His entire universe is bound together by the love of his parents for one another. For this loyalty to be disturbed is to shatter the child's universe into fragments. From that time on the child will be wary of all confidence and skeptical of all benignity. He will approach each new relationship armed with safeguards against skullduggery and deceit.

Many of today's adults have been thus disillusioned by the spiritual and actual infidelity of their parents. They were witnesses to bitter quarrels, tears and ruptures. They saw their fathers slam the front door and stalk angrily out of sight. They recall tearful notes, packed bags, and mothers' prolonged visits to relatives.

These are the children now grown up who close business deals, sign contracts, formulate laws, establish policies and marry. A lawyer's number is always in their phone book. Words are examined for deceit and contracts for loopholes. Clauses are inserted on paper and in their hearts that are evoked by premonitions of swindle, divorce, theft and betrayal. Everything must be written and an official seal affixed to guarantee prosecution if the party of the second part does a double-cross. This paranoia reaches its ultimate in the U. N., where every speech demands quadruplicate qualification and definition.

Marital infidelity is a disease of the smallest cells of the social body. Disintegration of the entire body can only be a matter of time. When society comes apart at the seams it comes apart at the family. Marital fidelity, by the same token, is the only cement strong enough to hold society together.

Dispositions to Infidelity

There are three basic causes of infidelity. The first is the modern ignorance of and lack of proper devotion to Mary. The second and third flow from the first: the immodesty of women and the dual morality of men.

In the nature things women play the supporting role in the family and consequently in society. Christianity confirms nature and recognizes this arrangement as judicious and satisfactory.

Human nature tends to degrade that which is subordinate. Those who are weak are most likely to be abused, whereas those who are strong and have social prestige can defend themselves. When Christianity made sacred a natural relationship between men and women in which the women became subordinate to the men, the relationship was modified by the fact that Christianity places Mary, a woman, as first among all created beings. Within the Christian context these two ideas are inseparable, that subordination is a means to the end of glorification, and the proof of that fact is Mary. The Christian home wherein the wife is subject to her husband also enshrines Mary as Queen of all created beings. The memory of Eve, whose feminine wiles persuaded Adam to sin, is erased by the presence of Mary, whose feminine docility made possible man's glorious redemption. Through Mary womanhood is lifted up for admiration, and it is woman's very selflessness and willing subservience which is the instrument of her glory. Seen in such a light subordination will never be degrading, but will possess instead the dignity of queenship.

When Protestantism rejected the theological doctrines concerning Mary and rooted out of their culture all reference to her, they inadvertently but inevitably degraded womanhood. They tried to retain the structure of the family without keeping the balance guaranteed by a love of Mary. The husbands at first became ruthless tyrants dominating the household. As Bible-thumping patriarchs they ruled the roost, providing women with only two alternatives: to be attractive but damned Jezebels, or else to be mousy matrons whose sole prerogative was to say "Amen" to their husbands' grace. Most significant in this tradition was the absence of any idea of feminine religious virginity. Dignity for women was something that could only be acquired by association with a husband, a brother, or a father. Apart from subservience to a man her life was meaningless.

This state of affairs could not continue for long because the shallow religious foundation upon which it was erroneously based rapidly fell apart. In the tradition of Mary, men and women *set one another free*. Through mutual love and the exercise of complementary talents each made it possible for the other to perform his or her vocation. The alternative to this mutual freedom is mutual slavery.

Mary had not only dignified womanhood, but by so doing had curbed the lusts of men, channelling passions in the direction of dedicated lives and good works. When she was ostracized, chastity went with her. Thus men became the slaves of women. Out of this emerged the two other dispositions to infidelity: feminine immodesty and the dual morality of men.

Immodesty

When feminine immodesty becomes a social institution, as it has today, it indicates an attempt on the part of women to gain the prestige, dominion and privilege which is their due, but to gain it without the price of dedication. The characteristic of such a plan is that emphasis on dress will be in the direction of the strange rather than the familiar. That is to say, strangeness (seductiveness) in the woman is precisely the opposite of the familiar, the family-ness, the *mother* or the *sister*. The mother and the sister are female types which are *dedicated,* one to her husband and family, and the other to God. This dedication provides them with a certain sexual immunity which is normally expressed in their manners and clothing. When I speak of sisters I mean unmarried virgins within or without religious orders. Remember that it is only within the two centuries that the manners and clothing of nuns and unmarried Christian women became remarkably dissimilar.

Other than the mother and the sister there is only the *strange* woman, the woman dedicated neither to God (with or without vows) nor to a husband and family. It is this strange woman who typifies and sets the style for all women today.

An excellent example of this can be given by contrasting the manner and dress of the average office girl with that of the average housewife. The housewife dresses throughout her workday to suit the nature of her work. She wears low-heeled comfortable shoes, a housedress which can take abuse and which permits freedom of movement for bending and lifting. She wears no jewelry for fear it might catch in something or become wet.

The office girl may do almost the same kind of work, that is to say, a manual effort of using her hands, bending, stooping, and walking. Yet her clothes are not at all prescribed by her work. She is forever breaking her over-long fingernails or chipping their paint. She is threatening the seams of her tight-fitting dresses, or catching frilly stuff on the corners of furniture. She totters around on high heels and splits her nylons bending to the files. Her pretty dresses are quickly soiled and wrinkled. Maintaining this costume, which is utterly awkward and unsuited to the work, takes a sizable portion, if not all, of her pay.

The reason for this madness is that the dedicated and familial type of womanhood no longer sets the style. The dress of the dedicated woman is prescribed by the function she performs. Today the strange woman sets the style. Every woman not a mother or a nun is per se a man-trap. That is the role to which society assigns her, pending the return of Mary.

Dual Morality

Men would not be so susceptible to feminine immodesty were it not for the fact that they have developed a double standard of morality. They have an entirely different "line" and approach for the mother-sister type than for the strange woman. They feel manfully responsible to open a door or pick up the gloves of a *good* woman, and yet they can laugh and joke and disparage the name of some *bad* woman, quite unconcerned as to whether she is receiving any gentlemanly consideration at all.

This dual morality has made men obtuse to various facts, such as:

1) Many young girls dress immodestly merely out of consent to the demands of fashion. The boundary line between dressing becomingly and dressing bewitchingly is not an easy one to survey, but the male instinct can detect quite readily all the styles that are south of the border. Many of those innocent young girls are unaware of the havoc they create in the male mind. They inadvertently arouse passions which they themselves would be most unwilling to satisfy. They precipitate infidelity and do not know it.

2) Strange women on the whole would be more than happy to become familial but are often prevented from doing so because of the attitude of *good* men who treat them as *bad* women. This was the theme of Philip Yordan's play *Anna Lucasta,* which was patterned (whether consciously or not I do not know) after the supernatural love of Christ for Mary Magdalene.

3) Many of today's sins of passion are provoked by the cold-blooded greed of landlords, price-fixers, entrepreneurs, magazine publishers, news distributors, fashion designers, store owners, *etc.* No Christian ethical code could justify placing those guilty of lust beyond the pale while those guilty of a more calculated greed remain inside. I hope that those who have by popular publishing introduced impure thoughts into the adolescent mind, or those who have demanded rents for hovels that despaired of becoming homes, will some night lose sufficient sleep to meditate for the first time on the many and devious ways there are for earning an honest buck in a society that cares nothing about the souls of *bad* people. I recall faintly the story of the Catholic distributor of spicy literature who said, "Of course, I wouldn't let *my* daughter read that stuff!" Dual morality with a vengeance!

4) A dual morality exists without reference to Mary. All persons should be treated with the same love and respect shown them by Christ. He died for them all, saints and sinners alike. The dual moralist has fallen for the strange woman whether he admits it even to himself. He would prefer rather that she remain available as a *bad* woman than that she be restored to Christ and thus be lost to him.

RESTORATION OF FIDELITY

Every material and spiritual aid rendered to the family in our times is an aid to restoring fidelity. Infidelity may come after the despair that follows a vain attempt to raise a family within a society that cares nothing about families. Above all, the restoration of feminine dignity is the primary aim. This can be best accomplished by reference to Mary. Her relation to the dignity of women in public life lies in her virginity. Her relation to the dignity of woman in private life lies in her motherhood.

It is not uncomplimentary to the opposite sex for a woman to reserve her most intimate love and affection for God alone. It was through just such an act of virginal love that Mary gained access to the treasury of graces that flow from her Son. She loved God so much and man so much that she refused herself to any one particular man as lover. She wished to remain open to the persuasion of grace and the calls of the needy undeterred by an attachment to one lover.

In our time there is a special need for this kind of love to bind men back to God. Devout women with a great capacity for sacrifice, immune to disappointments, finding consolation in their Beloved, are performing an apostolic function that no one else can do. Committed solely to Christ they can accomplish various acts of restoration which would be impossible for persons hampered by dependents or personal attachments. These women are the tangible evidence of the return of Mary to modern society. They represent the feminine potential of mankind realized in the dedication of full lives and services to the needs of the apostolate. Their fidelity to Christ provides a pattern of fidelity for the married to imitate.

Within the family the potency of Mary is again being felt. At Christian family meetings couples get together and the presence of the wives at the Gospel inquiry is a reminder that Mary sat so often with the first group of her Son's apostles. The brittle logic of the men is being modified and vitalized by the direct intuitive judgments of the women. A new and grand conception of motherhood is taking root. The queen of the household is coming to reign, belying the calumny that the role of housewife and mother is only for dopes and drudges.

Women in the home are imparting a new direction to the lives of their children. While men wrestle with Christian designs for a new society, the wives see already in the gestures and words of their children a new life growing in the awareness of the presence of Christ.

Marital fidelity will be restored, for Mary has come to live among us, showing us the glory of God that lies in a faithful heart.

Mothers-in-Law

Mary Reed Newland

"For this reason a man shall leave his father and mother, and shall cleave to his wife; and the two shall become one flesh."

So precisely put, it would seem of all relationships this one would know the least dissension. Yet because we are hearers of the word but not doers, there is strife and quarreling and unhappiness—and mother-in-law trouble. And as is his wont, when man is unable to cope with serious things he makes jokes about them. Poor joke, this. About as funny as the jokes on poverty and fecundity, youth and sex, riches and parsimony; travesties on the commands that we procreate, be pure, and love our neighbors as ourselves. Jokes about mother-in-law trouble are in the same category, dismissing as a comic maladjustment something that is tragic and which, if we are to restore ourselves as well as all things to Christ, is as needful of solution as all the social ills.

When we return to examine the command which has the most bearing upon it, we see it is not directed to the parents but to the newly-wedded pair, in order to impress upon them that once we marry we become masters of our new life in a special way. From the moment the vows are pronounced we are a unit, alone and committed to a course that has its start at the altar and its end in death. Perhaps some of the strife would have been avoided had it been di-

155

rected to the parents; but something so positive as a newly-made marriage calls for positive counsels—the relationships contingent to it are implied and are inevitable developments of these commands.

In its negative aspect, the new marriage might be viewed as one less under each parental roof, one less at each family board, so many less shirts or slips in each family wash. But it is infinitely more than that. It marks the completion of a vocation, and it marks the beginning of another. A sacred vocation, vested with such dignity that in the Gospels it is compared with the vocation of Christ as Head of His Church. Just as the mystical life of the Father and the Son are inseparably bound, yet separate, so is the life of the parent parting with the child through marriage. The same life is shared in essence, they are the same flesh, the love between them is everlastingly the same; yet as Christ's advent marked a coming forth from the Father, so the child comes forth from the house of his father and establishing himself in a new life is complete and dedicated in it. Again and again we see reflected the figure of the Mystical Body. First in the body itself: the body—head and members. Then in the family: "Wives be subject to your husbands as to the Lord; because a husband is head of the wife, just as Christ is head of the Church." Then in society: "Be subject to the higher authorities, for there exists no authority except from God." All nature, all human relationships, are designed to the same pattern—all echo the sacred dignity of Him Who is *the* Head—and in the affairs of men the type is established that we might achieve a likeness to it.

Where then does the trouble lie? Probably in a failure to appreciate what marriage is: a contract between three parties, man, woman and God—no one else. A poignant understanding of this should fill the bridal couple with such awe, with such jealousy for their newly-made maturity in God's eyes, that they would be loath to surrender any of their new prerogatives. And the parents, seeing the marriage in the stunning light of its sacramental reality, should fear so much as to reach out and lay a hand on it lest they mar the delicate balance which has been achieved at the altar and remains to be further consummated with physical and emotional and spiritual union.

At the wedding feast the new state of affairs is put sweetly, and usually sincerely, by the mother of the groom in terms of, "No, I don't feel I've lost a son, only gained a daughter." And yet it were better if she felt she *had* lost a son. For in truth she has. All but the ties of the flesh have been severed. She has the opportunity to surrender with grace, but if not, he is lost all the same. A renewal is stirring. Just as the vine dies in the winter after bearing its fruit, it is the fruit which starts again the following spring to bear and in another season to die. Somewhere along the way we have lost the sense of this immutable law—nature knows much more of surrender than we.

But what about a mother's "rights"? What are a mother's rights? "Honor thy father and thy mother." Marriage does not demand an end to the honoring. Honor and love are always due. With marriage, even more, even richer, for the entering into and sharing of the marriage state brings with it a new understanding of what the parents have done before. And the parents, in turn, receive the honor with a new graciousness, not in the same sense as when it came from the child, but coming from adults who are better able to see the warp and woof of the years' struggles, who see for the first time the pattern of their sacrifices, and whose love is less voluble, more fervent. These are the gifts of honor and love in their richest raiment. Again not defined but implicit, divinely designed to fill the needs of those whose fulfillment rests now, having completed the first cycle of their vocation, on surrendering to the abatement of physical stamina, on looking ahead to the end of life, the beginning of eternity. Now is the time for watching the growth and flowering of what seeds have been sown. We sow the Word within the flesh of our own, and the time comes when the work is done.

When this sense of the sanctity of the bridal role is lacking, it is usually not through any conscious fault, but rather because we have humanized everything about us, marriage included. Not that it is unnatural, un-human—but in order even to be, it must first be *super*natural. It so often becomes solely a cozy event, and a happy one, and to be told it is a noble and high vocation, that mutual sanctification of the partners and the sanctification of their offspring is the goal are nice words, even familiar words, but they no longer seem to etch the consciousness with a profound understanding of what has been started with the first step into marriage.

THE HUSBAND HOLDS THE KEY

It is in proportion to his awareness of these things that the husband leaves the door closed, ajar or wide open to the overpossessiveness and interference by parents. No amount of citing texts seems able to override this blindness where it exists. A cloud of sentimentality settles down like a fog over his judgments, and he is unable to draw clearly lines past which no one, even his beloved parents, may trespass. We say husband as though the shoe were never on the other foot, when of course it is many times. But since the role of head of the family casts upon his shoulders the larger burden of maintaining its confines sacred, his is the larger responsibility in this charge. The wife has many and equally solemn responsibilities, and the vision should be shared by both, but he is the spokesman and he it is who is usually at fault in the business of mother-in-law trouble. He it is who suffers such a ravishment of husbandly dignity when interferences are countenanced, for if he is not to fulfill this first charge with vigor, then all other things stand chance of failing in the wake of this first failure. And the number of marriages is legion where interference by mothers-in-law has driven a wedge in the intimate union of mind and body which must exist if there is to be a sense of the wholeness of the union, a togetherness in all things.

So far, so good. The husband has a definite stand which he must take, not just because he must be nice to his wife, but because God has made it his sacred obligation. The proper climate for fulfillment depends on erecting certain protective barriers around his marriage, and even the physical fulfillment in marriage can be marred by interference. It can be insisted to the point of vocal paralysis that physical fulfillment is the essence, and to "live," physical compatibility alone is the must—and one can answer that for those to whom marriage is nothing more than physical union, delightful as it may be, living has not yet begun. Over and over we are told it is the mind of Christ which must be in us—it is the mind of Christ which is the life of the members of His Body. We can be united to Him in His Church, but if we are not of His mind we are dead branches on a tree. And so in marriage, we can be united in physical union to the point of satiety and if there is no union of minds and spirits, there is far short of perfect fulfillment. In truth there is already the cancer sown whereby even the physical union can pall and eventually kill. That these parallels exist is not accidental. That the figure of Christ as the Bridegroom and the Church as His Bride are compared to the figures of the man and woman united in matrimony is not simply pretty poetry. There is even the awful evidence of schism to point a parallel to the awful interference of those outside the married couple. We know by what rule of faith we must live to safeguard faith, and we are shown by what rule of union we must live to safeguard the sanctity of the marriage.

Many times, however, even when the husband makes clear his impeccable loyalty to this obligation, there is still strife—the result of personalities at war with one another regardless of what lines are drawn, what loyalties declared. And in this case, the burden of solution is the wife's. To be told by a son that you may not interfere is not guaranteed to make a mother-in-law automatically fall in love with her daughter-in-law. Quite the contrary, it is practically certain to widen the chasm between them. And the unhappiness resulting can be just as corrosive as the other type of interference.

The great paradox of Christianity is a setting up of boundaries and confines with truth, and a reaching over and beyond them with love. Christ hates sin, loves the sinner; His Church hates error, loves the erring. So in marriage; where there is incompatibility of temperament between herself and her mother-in-law, the wife hates the discord, but must love the discordant. And we say *must* advisedly, for we are bound by His love on the Cross to love the same way.

THE WIFE UNDERSTANDS

So, having seen a conflict set up by the definition of her role as mistress of her own household, a wife is bound to set about the task of making her mother-in-law love her in spite of it. She never will *because* of it. And this is hard. Hard for both (obviously the command to love applies to both) but possibly not as hard for the wife as for the mother-in-law. The younger woman is more facile usually; her outlook is colored by her youthfulness of mind and body, she is setting out upon a course which promises to be exciting and full of adventure. The older woman has met and solved her problems as a wife and mother, she has formed opinions and habits, she has put years between herself and the bride she once was, and her ability to return to know the mind of her youth is limited. She sees her experience and her knowledge as short-cuts by which she may save the young wife needless waste of time and effort; she fails to see, or is incapable of seeing, that part of the growth and maturity of the younger woman depends upon being left alone to make her way by trial and error. This is not to say that the parents can never profit the young couple by their own experience; but more often than not, the young people can best learn by making their own mistakes.

All this a young woman may come to understand, and it is armed with her understanding of this, with complete honesty, and with the love that is Christ's, that a young wife tackles the task of learning to love a difficult mother-in-law and waiting to see her love returned. There are few rules, there is no magic. It is a long, slow, often painful process. If young wives were saints, it would be easier—but they have themselves to conquer in order to win their mothers-in-law. They must learn a beautiful patience, they must evaluate actions and motives with simple honesty. They must understand, first of all, that surrender for the older woman is very difficult—not because of intractable character necessarily, but because she is harnessed by years of habit. Saving face is one of the most fundamental of human conceits, and the young wife starts her married life with no face to save, if we may put it that way, but her mother-in-law has erected a whole hierarchy of values which, even though some are outdated, are for her the rule, and surrendering them to innovation demands much humility and graciousness. This cannot be done overnight. Where the conflict exists it is as concrete, as tangible, as oil and water unmixed. To resort to the technical jargon of our day, it is a homogenization of the two personalities which must be accomplished to achieve the solution.

CHRIST LOVES

It does no good for the young wife to consider what are, for her, her mother-in-law's faults and try to overcome her impatience with them. She must start far before that. She must start at the point where she sees in her mother-in-law one whom Christ finds infinitely lovable, for whom He paid His precious price on the Cross, and who, in a mysterious way, is to Him as the only one. When we are faced with problems of incompatibility, so often we picture ourselves reflecting the injustices suffered by Christ; we offer them up with all the nobility we can muster and in a sweet, sticky puddle of self-pity extend the wound for more salt. It comes as a shock when we discover that our adversary offers up the conflict in the same terms. And usually that is the beginning of honesty—of a soundly humble evaluation of the unhappy state of affairs. For Christ would be with both, and should He chide, it would not be with a listing of faults and an exhortation to mend ways, but with "Love one another as I love you." It is impossible to strip the ego down to its proper puny size any other way, and it is equally impossible to find any other motive for trying to love someone who is really hard for you to love. This knowledge, that love is possible through Him, and that we will receive the grace to accomplish it from Him, does much to reduce tension and relax a soul faced with a long, slow, patient trek toward achievement. And it would seem the only rule to be applied universally for in-laws who have trouble loving one another is to keep the gaze fixed on Christ. This, and much prayer, will light the first tiny flame and it will grow as it feeds on grace.

The plea to love is a fine high-sounding ideal, and we can swallow it in terms of loving someone who is out of reach and whose enmity is on the grand scale, but when it takes the form of little irritations, daily annoyances, it is much much harder. Remember in *The Brothers Karamazov* the elder, Father Zossima, says of love: "Active love is labor and fortitude, and for some people too, perhaps, a complete science. But I predict that just when you see with horror that in spite of all your efforts you are getting further from your goal instead of nearer to it—at that very moment I predict that you will reach it and behold clearly the miraculous power of the Lord Who has been all the time loving and mysteriously guiding you." And so if we are going to be saints, we who are married, it is going to be not only by loving our vocation, but also loving those who, because of it, are right under our noses, whose rattling of pots and pans and slamming of doors sets our nerves on edge, whose ceaseless advice and correction become a cross almost too heavy to bear.

STAY WITH IT

We have said there is no magic formula, but there are snares of which we can beware. One of the few comforts which *seems* justified for the young woman weighed down by mother-in-law trouble is running to her own people with her tale of woe. There she receives the comfort and understanding she needs, so she thinks, and yet very rarely is anything positive accomplished by it. And surely something negative is: a further erection of resistance and barriers. She returns, relieved of her burden, inspired to vindicate herself, armed with a refreshed stubbornness, resentment, and her head full of reviewed "rights" by which she will be vindicated. When what is needed is love and understanding and tenderness, these sorties to the old stamping grounds are to be avoided like the plague.

And in the same sense, exchange of notes about the persecutions of mothers-in-law with other women who suffer the same trials are rarely worthwhile. If one is aiming at love as the only solution, and it *is* the only solution, every little breach of loyalty to the intimate family circle is an eating away of the honest effort already made. And don't we all know, too well, how after having surmounted some problem of human relationships at last, we look back at our own smallness in having discussed the problem with outsiders and burn with shame at the memory of it?

Then there is this last consideration: for the married, everyone who is part of their life is there by the knowledge and consent of God. One might even be so bold as to say for the married, it takes in-laws as well as husbands and children to mix a recipe for the way to perfection. St. Monica found it so. It would be a comfort and a help if instead of running to mothers to pour out the miseries young wives would run to the *Confessions* of St. Augustine. There they will find his account of how Monica, his mother, ran headlong into a mother-in-law bent upon persecution, and how with patience and love and prayer, by trying to serve instead of trying to fight, she won the older woman's fierce devotion—and of course in the end, that high, high sanctity for herself that is the destination for all of us.

THE SPIRITUALITY OF MARRIED LIFE

Elizabeth M. Sheehan

The daily sacrifices, trials and monotonies of life must be seen under the light of a certain spirit, not that of the world. Charity plays an underrated part in the spirituality of married life.

I remember a certain street corner where I stood for many nights waiting for the bus after work. Across from me, in some kind of mean dwelling, I used to see through the window a sort of home, poor and bare, but glowing like a beacon out of the weary dusk. Within that small circle of light the table would be laid, the meal in readiness for someone. I cannot forget the keen sense of incompleteness that would sweep over me at that bus stop. I saw my own life as the broken arc of that warm circle and all the longing for someone to share, not merely ideas, but life itself was summed up in that little scene.

Time and again I have seen in women the subtle attack of that loneliness common in varying degrees to all mankind. This peculiar type may begin with the night-fall ache, when all the day's hopes have been plundered, the mightiest conquests sink into inconsequence, the liveliest prospects blow through the spirit like a drift of dead leaves. Gradually the damp fog of loneliness, poignant at times and at times merely stifling, closes in on either side till it reaches the morning, stands at the bedside ready to greet one on waking.

Why is this paralyzing loneliness so widespread among women of our time? Perhaps it is because so many of us sometimes do not realize in time that while a career may demand all our strength, time, talents and endurance, only a vocation can possess the heart.

And it is just this which we, as women, long above all to give. God in His Providence, while bestowing upon man and woman similar intellectual powers, did not give woman that special drive which enables man to continue putting the things of the mind in first place. This blessed shortcoming of women is what has always held Christian homes together, developed religious vocations, and brought saints into the world.

For this reason, and because they find it more difficult to approach God directly, most women find the solace to their peculiar loneliness and the pathway to salvation in the vocation of marriage.

MARRIAGE IN CHRIST

We all know the essential doctrine concerning Christian marriage. We know that the sacred bond was instituted by God on the sixth day of creation. Even before his nature had been tainted by the first sin, man evidently could have suffered from loneliness, a loneliness which might have been even greater because of the acuity of all his powers.

"And the Lord said: It is not good for man to be alone; let us make him a helpmate like unto himself."

The union of Adam and Eve therefore was blessed with the marks of unity, perpetuity and indissolubility that have always distinguished Christian marriage. That first union has been considered as a divine foreshadowing of the Incarnation. It shows clearly that marriage cannot in any sense be considered a concession to weakness because it was founded in Paradise.

In the chaos which followed the Fall and the subsequent corruption of marriage among Jews and Gentiles, God never revoked the blessing He had originally granted, that blessing "which alone was not taken away either by the punishment for original sin or by the sentence of the flood."

The coming of Christ gave marriage a new dignity and made it a sacrament. Christ by His presence at Cana and the performance of His first miracle there, gave marriage added holiness. Thus Pope Leo XIII tells us, in his Encyclical *Arcanum Divinae,* that Christ "in a wondrous way, making marriage an example of the mystical union between Himself and His Church, not only perfected that love which is according to nature, but also made the natural union of one man with one woman far more perfect through the bond of heavenly love."

In the Gospels, Our Lord likened the Kingdom of Heaven to a marriage feast, and in His preaching He restored the holiness, unity and perpetuity of the bond.

St. Paul, in his turn, calls marriage "a great sacrament." His explanation of it in the Epistle to the Ephesians is familiar to all. He compares it again to the Mystical Union of Christ with the Church, a concept whose sublimity we can but dimly grasp when we meditate on the Canticle of Canticles. Here the Holy Ghost, inspiring Solomon, took the symbol of marriage as the example of Christ's love for the Church, the chosen souls, and particularly Mary, the Immaculate Conception. "Thou art all fair, O my love," He sings to her, "and there is not a spot in thee."

Mystics often have used the language of connubial love which, though it must fall infinitely short of its burden, nevertheless seems to be the sole means of conveying in language something of the raptures of divine love.

Thus we see that Christian marriage is intrinsically holy by reason of its having God as its Author and because Christ made it a sacrament and a symbol of His own love.

What Is This Vocation?

Such is the dignity of the vocation to which most of us are called. But, we may ask, does not love for another person necessarily lessen our love for Almighty God?

This is the very secret of the true love between man and wife. Oriented toward God as their final end, both man and woman must see in the partner not a destination but a helper, a companion along the road to eternity. It is when the exchange of love is immanent between the two that marriages must fail. If the union is to be spiritually fruitful, the love of both must be turned to God. Hence the analogy St. Paul makes: The man represents Christ, the woman the Church, the love between them, the Holy Ghost, as the love between the first and second Persons of the Holy Trinity. "Husbands, love your wives, as Christ also loved the Church and delivered Himself up for it."

This passage of love is clearly seen at the altar railing. Here the man and woman do not face one another. They kneel, side by side, before God. So should it be throughout life, looking to Him, not to one another, for their ultimate sustenance, both material and spiritual. They must see God in and through one another, not each other as gods. Then the discovery of the inevitable imperfection will not bring disillusion, which comes when that gaze of the soul which seeks to rest in divinity discovers in its object only the shortcomings of its own nature.

Again, according to that high dignity St. Paul gives to the relationship, the man is to his wife in some way as God to the soul. What is God's Will for each soul? Its sanctification. What is Christ's Will for His Church? His sacrifice was made "that he might sanctify it...that he might present it to himself, a glorious church, not having spot or wrinkle or any such thing: but that it should be holy and without blemish."

Can we not then attribute to the Christian husband a certain responsibility, a loving solicitude for the soul of his wife? We know now what manner of love this should be.

THE MEETING OF TWO MYSTERIES

But in such a union there can be no question of possession. The partners in marriage do not *own* one another. Even in the intimate embrace of life together, surrendering and sacrificing certain of their rights one to another for the sake of children and mutual faith, they must never forget the mystery of each other's souls. How easily we can understand the despair that soon overtakes those who look to the physical union as the most complete, for as the Apostle says, "The wisdom of the flesh is death, but the wisdom of the spirit is life and peace." And the desire of the flesh, imperious though it be, is after all so much less than the desire of the heart, which can rest in God alone.

No, the true union in marriage is a union of souls, as Pius XI says clearly in his Encyclical *Casti Connubii*:

> By matrimony, therefore, the souls of the contracting parties are joined and knit together more directly and more intimately than are their bodies, and that not by any passing affection of sense or spirit, but by a deliberate and firm act of the will; and from this union of souls by God's decree, a sacred and inviolable bond arises.

It is the souls, each one harkening to its own vocation, that is, God's call, each one pursuing its own destiny, which must be joined. But joined not by ties of perfect understanding (for we can never completely understand another) but by ties of perfect charity. Charity does not seek to possess. It is a union strong in tenderness and concern, yet it is infinitely light, delicate and unbinding, the merest touch.

For in each life are two continual and concurrent conversations, the conversation with men and the conversation with God. The religious foregoes the conversation with men to listen with full attention to the divine voice. For those who find their vocation in marriage, these two conversations must proceed side by side, never conflicting, and, as it were, never meeting.

"As God to the soul." The loved one must always be left free. God, while loving each soul with an infinite love and desiring its sanctification, nevertheless leaves the will of each person free to turn to Him or not. Perhaps this is why the love of such a one as the Little Flower delights Him so that He showers miraculous gifts of grace upon her. She is one who realizing her freedom, turned to Him with all her powers. Love, she knew, is a gift. It is made up of thousands of little courtesies, thousands of little and big sacrifices and offerings of oneself gladly rendered. Love anticipates the least will of the beloved. It cannot be forced. The lover does not rudely grasp the will of is beloved. He leaves it free, delighting and exulting all the ore if it turns toward him, hoping, praying, patiently and gently beckoning should it seem to turn away.

The Way of Salvation

When we meditate on this holy gift of matrimony, we come once more to the boundless mercy of Divine Providence. Consider for a moment how every will created has been stiffened by original sin and its own subsequent wanderings. How few would be bent back to their Creator, would grasp fully the mystery of the Unseen Reality, by knowledge alone. Love, on the other hand, is easy for us. It ennobles

the dullest understanding. God therefore opened the way to
salvation through love, and through love of another creature.
He made marriage so that through loving one who would
be beside us at all times in everyday life, ready to comfort,
help and support us, one whom we can see with our natural
powers and who arouses in us natural affection, we could
also gain eternal life.

Does it sound too simple? Let us remember it is never
going to be easy. The young girl at the altar, resplendent in
the purity of her bridal gown, may believe she is entering
upon an earthly paradise. Young hopes and innocence light
her eyes. Perhaps it is just as well she does not see all that
she is choosing.

But that woman who kneels in the back of the church
in her shabby coat, the tired one with lines of worry on her
face. She jabs at the tears with a rumpled handkerchief. She is
ashamed to be always caught crying at weddings. She knows
what the vocation of a wife and mother really is. Glorious,
to be sure, and full of its peculiar joys. But full likewise of
its peculiar sufferings, sickness, disappointments, anxieties
and failures, annoyances, monotonies, and all of it.

The bride whose voice is so tremulous as she pronounces
those words that bind soul to soul, "I plight unto thee my
troth,"—is it right to darken such a glorious morning with
the somber shadow of sufferings to come? The woman in the
back of the church could tell us it is far better to understand
the meaning of tears.

What was Our Lord's answer when He was asked about
the highest vocation? The Cross. There are countless wives
and mothers who have learned to understand and accept this
profound truth, as they followed Him as best they could,
through dreary daily routines, piles of dirty clothes, jangling

telephones, nights of sickbed vigil, scraping up money for the bills, misunderstandings and the rest.

For in choosing a vocation (Should we not rather say in *being* chosen?) we choose our particular vale of tears. The ordinary way of sanctification is through accepting the sacrifices and sufferings of daily life. The discipline of life together can serve ultimately the same purpose as the rule of the religious in stamping out self-will and pride. The Trappist rising at night to praise God on the cold stones, the mother rising to minister to a sick child, can both be doing the same thing—the *Opus Dei.*

"Happy the bride the sun shines on" runs the old adage. But if we take that sun to be the Sun of Grace, Christ our Lord, then happy indeed! For the chief gift that the bride and groom bear away from the altar on the wedding morning is a key to the Communion of Saints. Marriage the sacrament, by divine generosity, has thrown open to one weak man and one weak woman one of the seven great doors to the inexhaustible treasuries of grace.

From that time forward, every act she performs as a wife and mother, every act he performs as a husband and father can be lightened by that Sun. And it will be precisely according to their response to these offerings of grace as wife or husband, and no longer as individuals, that each one will gain salvation. That is the meaning of vocation.

For hard days to come, both have the consolation of the divine promise that to those who will accept them, He will give, and in abundance, all the graces necessary to fulfill the duties of that life for which He has chosen them and in which He has united them. Graces for the temptations that may come from the world, from their own weakness, from the evil one. Graces for the temptations to despair when the going gets too rough, when hardships multiply;

graces to bear up under financial strains, the handicaps of ill health, the inevitable differences of opinion. Graces, even, to find God merciful should He take to heaven their newly baptized firstborn child. Graces to turn aside peaceably from the sharp tongue of the neighbor who cannot see how they can afford another baby.

What about the other side of the picture, the possible failures, possible lack of faith? We know the answer, though it is harder to accept. Even if the Church for grave reason should allow the wife, for example, to live apart from her husband, still the Church cannot dissolve the bond that unites them spiritually. This bond entails a certain lasting responsibility for her husband's salvation, no matter how erring and unjust he may be. Her life, though it be a martyrdom by human standards, must then be devoted to winning him the necessary graces to gain heaven; tears, prayers, penances—the vocation of so many saintly women. Yes, these too must come under the heading, "graces of the sacrament." And very often the outcome of the tragedy is triumph, but only when the cares of this life are ended. Such is the meaning of the big word "indissoluble."

What God has joined He has joined for the salvation of both of them!

The Other Half

This brings us to the source of so many difficulties today, marriages grounded on the rocks instead of on the Rock because of pitiable fads in choosing one's life partner. Not only is this done too often carelessly, but by such absurd standards as are certain to prove false and ephemeral under the stress of life. All sorts of circumstances may enter into it, future business prospects, "personality," money, and so on, down to height, color of eyes, and preferences in music!

How novel and revolutionary it would be to ask instead: Is this the man whom God created to help me save my soul? Is he aware of his obligation to become a saint and to help me become one? Yes, it is true to say that, since it is a supernatural love between them, the wife has more right to expect her husband to possess the gifts and fruits of the Holy Ghost than money in the bank.

"Be careful," warn the experts, "this is for life!" But life itself, fifty or sixty years, is but a passing moment. The relative merits of a fifteen thousand dollar house versus a shabby flat, a new car versus a crowded bus, fade instantly into oblivion in the sharp glare of eternity.

It is, in a sense, a choice beyond time. "Till death do us part," but it is not over then. The physical presence of the loved one must be foregone. But this soul to which your soul is bound fast in a knot no human agency, not time itself, can dissolve. Are you not more concerned over whether it will see God than whether it will enjoy the benefits of an all-electric kitchen?

> This mutual inward moulding of husband and wife, this determined effort to perfect each other, can in a very real sense, as the Roman Catechism teaches, be said to be the chief reason and purpose of matrimony. (Encyclical *Casti Connubii*)

Some spiritual writer has said that it is seldom that a man goes to heaven unaccompanied by his wife. This gives some idea of the terrible significance of this union we call marriage. Perhaps we allow its social aspects, important though they be, to overshadow its spiritual aspect. Still, it is good to have the eternal view of things as much as we can. Then we see readily that in a sense only a man on the point of death experiences the fullness of life. So in the same way we can make the best decisions about this life from the viewpoint of its finish.

We say then to the young girl choosing her partner for eternity: Do not look to Hollywood to make up your mind. Do not even accept the friendly, well-meaning advice of those around you, if you suspect they would chiefly like to see you nicely situated in a suburban sort of way. Do not consult public opinion, powerful though it be. Consult the Holy Ghost. It is an awful decision and should be made with the help of prayer. The views of all these people, the pressing standards of this world, the humiliations of poverty or lowliness, are as nothing before the staggering prospect of eternity. Above all, we beg, do not close your eyes to the fact that it is not merely life you will be sharing, but death. The finality of this decision is described by Alice Meynell:

> O rash! (I smile) to pledge my hidden wheat.
> I fold today at altars far apart
> Hands trembling with what toils? In their retreat
> I seal my love-to-be, my folded art.
> I light the tapers at my head and feet,
> And lay the crucifix on this silent heart.

It is strange, but when you meditate on the death of the beloved, you see immediately the fitness or unfitness of the union, for there will lie the anchor or despair of your own soul.

To say that life together must be grounded on the fact of death brings us to the question of joy. For death is the end of the hard earthly journey and the beginning of eternal joy. Are the trials and tribulations of this time of such great moment after all? Are any hardships comparable to the joys that are to come? No, eye has not seen, nor ear heard! Would we ever do anything that would in the least endanger that joy for someone we love?

Bring it down to everyday life. Would we ever forego the sharp answer, forebear the pain and weariness, if we saw how we can help or hinder the gaining of that joy? How good it is to know that all the events of today that seem so pressing, so urgent, will tomorrow be less than the wind that bends the grass!

THE DAILY ROUND

It is only under this light that the daily sacrifices of life together, the trials and monotonies, become not only meaningful helps toward salvation but sources of joy that can indeed foreshadow the unending joys of heaven. For by charity, it is said, we can taste heaven while still on earth.

Let us look at these acts we perform every day, acts in themselves dull or indifferent, costing us much effort or little. Let us see them not merely as concessions to some human need or weakness, some human whim perhaps, but as a stepping-stone toward mutual salvation.

Looking at life in this way, a Christian wife will want to make the home not only orderly and attractive, she will try to create an atmosphere which will draw her husband and children away from the world, toward God. The home itself, kindergarten of heaven, should always reflect clearly its sublime purpose. It should contain religious pictures and symbols. It should never overstress material comforts. Its latchkey should be the Cross. Its warmth the charity of the Holy Spirit. Christ the Cornerstone. Every Christian homemaker will honor as her model the simplicity, the poverty, the mutual love and protection of the Holy Family of Nazareth. Quite evidently this was God's plan for a happy marriage. What other ideal could there possibly be for us?

And the husband and wife—should they not minister to one another's spiritual needs as well as the material? It can become very real. They are supposed to sustain one another's faith. Where one falters, God gives the other grace to support. Where one cannot accept suffering, the other must try to reach it. Where one might be tempted to make a decision of reason, a decision of the world, the other is there to remind them of spiritual values. They must help one another to practice the works of mercy, not only in respect to the members of their own immediate household, but in respect to the members of that larger household, the Mystical Body. They must learn to preface their plans for the future with the phrase "if God wills."

Thus the routine of family life observed with patient, loving effort year after year can take away our pride, our worldly values. It can transfer our attention from ourselves to the needs of others. It can destroy selfishness. It teaches us to accept suffering and privation, all under the sweet yoke of love. It inculcates resignation, patience, humility, referring all things to God for their eventual outcome and purpose.

Of course, the family will pray together. Husband and wife have turned their souls toward God together. They are dedicated to the task of raising up saints to Him. There will be daily Mass and the reception of the sacraments together whenever possible. The haste of life is not too hasty for grace at meals, the Angelus in the morning, perhaps a few minutes of spiritual reading in common at some quiet time of the day. When circumstances permit, a retreat or day of recollection, together if possible, will renew the luster of the wedding day. Every day, we can each try to offer up our everyday sacrifices in the morning and think of that offering as often as possible through the day.

Particularly, we can bring each day, with all its assorted joys and troubles, to a full circle in the evening Rosary together. Perhaps we are too tired to meditate on the Mysteries as they should be meditated upon. But let us try to put the weariness of today and the threat of tomorrow aside for a while. Let us remember that we are all little children before God, and it is He, especially through Mary, the Blessed

Mother of His own Household, Who can sanctify our life together.

THE TRAGEDY OF
MODERN WOMAN

Carol Jackson

Something has been lost in recent times. Women have often borne the brunt of some of the most serious social changes. In what does a woman truly find fulfillment?

WHAT WOMEN WANT

If you want to take the measure of modern society in terms of human happiness, watch the faces of the women. The female of our species is much more sensitive than the male to the things of the spirit, and whatever she feels, and is, will be written on her face after the age of twenty-five or thirty. We are so fashion-conscious that we seldom even look at the soul of modern woman as revealed by her eyes and the lines of her face. In this way we miss observing that most American women, those emancipated and lovely ladies of commercial fiction, either cry themselves to sleep every night or are past giving way to the sorrow and frustration that encompasses them.

The nature of woman is a matter for philosophical and spiritual investigation. No Gallup poll is needed, or would even be useful, in finding out what women are made for. They are made as all human beings (men included) for God, both here and hereafter. But in a special way women are destined for love and service; love and service of God, usually in the person of another human being. It can be stated dogmatically that the key to any woman's character, and to her happiness or unhappiness, lies in discovering *whom* she loves, whereas a man, though he shares ultimately the same destiny, is frequently caught loving a yacht or a car or a corporation.

In respect to a woman's loves, she will be happy if they are rightly ordered and duly reciprocated, miserable otherwise. Rightly ordered means that God will get her first love and that all her other loves will be somehow in Christ. In this light one can examine modern woman and see that our society has betrayed her on every level.

The Tragedy of Wasted Sacrifice

The tragedy of the aging woman with grown-up children today is the tragedy of wasted sacrifice. In God's plan marriage is intended to be the path of sanctification for most women, the altar of daily sacrifice made easy by love. Marriage is so natural a vehicle for dying to oneself that even today it is rare to see a married woman who is selfish unless she has refused through contraception to permit the ordinary fructification of marriage. A woman with a child immediately takes on a dignity, a dignity which increases as the family grows and the sacrifices multiply. The normal woman, be she Christian or pagan, gives to her children before herself. They are well clothed while she gets shabbier; they attend school at the expense of new furniture or perfume. The normal woman does not even notice her sacrifices because she loves her children and is surrounded by their need for her.

So far it is all part of God's plan. It is all a prelude to joy unceasing. It is a sort of purgatorial stage of the spiritual life to act as a prelude to the joys of union with God. A Christian woman, while loving her husband and children, should grow increasingly eager for what popular psychologists, with their foolish terminology, call the "empty nest" period, when the house is deserted and the children all at college or married. She should be eager because she should be pretty well stripped of self-love and ready for a swift progress in the spiritual life once she is free for more prayer. She should be already far enough advanced spiritually to count past sacrifices as nothing and to hope she can soon live a more penitential, frugal, simple, and contemplative life than has been possible with a growing family around. Like the saint queens of hagiography she should be planning the personal service she will give to the sick or the needy when her hands are free to love Christ in His least lovable.

The tragedy of the middle-aged American woman whom God intended thus to sanctify hits you with full force if you listen to any of the radio give-away programs. They represent a mountainous vulgarity, a truly shameful indignity. But slightly less vulgarly the same tragedy extends to the more refined suburbanites who waste their declining years in bridge, travel and gossip.

Everyone cooperates in making sure that the years of sacrifice do not fructify. "Now you can have your new car, your trip to Bermuda, your hair elegantly done, the latest dish washing machine and fine clothes!" scream the advertisements, seconded by public opinion. What they are really saying is, "Now that you have been at least partially stripped of self-love, you can learn to love yourself again, so that you may be able to lose your soul after all, and if you don't lose your soul you can at least have the opportunity of going through the stripping all over again, and in a much more painful way, in purgatory."

Husbands only serve to heighten the tragedy, although for other reasons. Owing to a distorted ideal of married love (more about this later), it is considered today that a woman must hold her husband's affection by her physical charms. How cruel the world's way is, compared to God's. In God's plan a man and his wife would so have grown in spiritual unity by middle age that the most beautiful eighteen-year-old secretary, despite her evident charms, would fail to hold the husband's attention. In the world's scheme love never deepens. It's always superficial and physical. This imposes a torture on all middle-aged women whose waist lines finally expand beyond all repressing and who look more and more pathetic in their determined youthfulness. They must always be dieting when they would otherwise (had they been nearing the goal of holiness) be fasting. They suffer doubly because they will not accept suffering. They are vastly more lonely for having turned away from solitude. The devil is a hard task master.

THE TRAGEDY OF HALF-GIVING

The tragedy of half-giving stalks the unmarried women who are not nuns. Perhaps the best way to see their plight is within an historical perspective.

The single state is, strictly speaking, unnatural. It is tolerable and significant (as will be shown) only within a Christian context where it can be raised to a supernatural role. Pagan societies never tolerated single women (as a class, that is; there were accidental special cases). They were pressed into concubinage or prostitution. One of the most notable social effects of Christianity was that it provided a status and function to unmarried women. They would be "brides of Christ," women who were impatient of reaching their final goal of divine love through the intermediary channel of human love and so chose a direct route of total and immediate self-giving to God, either in a life stripped of all but the barest necessary activities for the sake of contemplation or within the framework of a religious order devoted to the works of mercy. As brides of Christ these women were able to love as fully as possible, and their love overflowed all over Europe in the service of the poor and the sick, the homeless, the leper and the ignorant. Peace and joy characterized their countenances, and people said of them then as they say of them now, "You can never tell how old a nun is—they always look young."

The Protestant Reformation dispensed with nuns, totally in some countries, partially in others. But Protestantism couldn't erase the memory of the freedom not to marry, nor the ideal of free service in the works of mercy. The last several centuries have witnessed the progressive deterioration of the status of the single woman as she was divorced progressively from her role of Christ's spouse. We still have vestiges of the tail end of that regression in the "noble humanitarian" maiden lady who was popularly called an "old maid." Popular appellations are usually somewhat accurate, even if cruel. No one would ever have called a nun an old maid. It was the secular spinster who had withered up because she couldn't love fully and give her service wholly. And now we see the final decay of half-giving. Teachers, nurses and social workers, divorced from Christ except accidentally (where they are pious on the side but do not see Christ in the patient or the student or client, or if they do are caught up in a system which doesn't corroborate their findings), are sick of half-giving, of leading lonely if useful lives, and are capitulating to self-seeking. They are all asking for more money, not knowing that their frustration comes from quite another source and that they are but jumping from unhappiness to ruination.

Career Girls

Career girls are another facet of the unmarried woman problem, descended in an indirect line by way of the emancipation of woman. They are not wholly the termini of the secularized nun but are caught up equally with the disgruntled wife. Without tracing their ancestry in detail, let us examine their present plight.

It can be said categorically that the career girl *cannot* be happy (that is as a career girl–she may accidentally be fulfilled because her career is secondary to the support of an aged mother or a brother studying for the priesthood, or because she only works for a little while and finds it exciting). You have only to ask one question to see why. *Whom* does a career girl love? As a woman she must love *someone* wholly.

She does not love God, not enough anyhow. That is apparent by definition. A career girl is one who is forging a place for herself in business, government, the arts–some secular activity. It does not involve a religious dedication. God, then, is out as the center of her life.

Most career girls try to go against their natures. They pretend that they can make themselves like men, impersonal, objective, happy in the pursuit of things. If they have love affairs they try to make them seem casual, as though their hearts were not involved. The more glittering a woman's career (in the eyes of the world) the more apt the woman herself is to be distorted, unhappy and neurotic.

Then there are a multitude of career girls who love their bosses, knowingly or unknowingly, morally or immorally, with home-breaking effects or not. It is not in a woman to give her total service and dedication to the Amalgamated Pickle Company or National Horseshoes, Inc., without having a personal attachment involved. Business tends to exploit this fact because it is to the interest of the firm to have devoted workers, and if a roomful of girls is going to be asked to work late night after night it is useful to have a handsome personnel manager. The situation is especially acute in the case of secretaries so aptly named "office wives." Night after night, from coast to coast, important Mr. Jones leaves the office early for golf and then cocktails and dinner, while Mary Jane Smith works on until 8:00 P.M. cleaning up the mail. Often enough she doesn't know why she does it, and most often too Mr. Jones is obtuse enough to accept the sacrifice without realizing its disorienting effects on Mary Jane's life.

The only way for a determined career girl to escape from the emotional disorders which beset her is for her to give all her love to someone whose interests are identical with her own, that is, herself. Needless to say, self-love is to the self's ultimate destruction, but it seemingly frees people from being hurt by others (the person you love always has the power to hurt you). When a career woman thus "frees" herself by loving only herself she becomes a ruthless creature who terrifies all around her. A calloused male, seeking money or power, is warm and human by contrast. And, needless to say, such a woman is in a far more perilous state as regards her soul than the secretary she makes miserable and the operator who is secretly in love with the head bookkeeper.

THE LAY APOSTLE

Single women must again turn to Christ with a total love and service. It is easy to say that they ought to marry or enter the convent, but that is often not the answer. Neither is it the answer for them to continue their secular course and pile up novenas on the side. Today's answer to the problem of the single girl is usually the lay apostolate, some form of Catholic Action which will give her a Christ-centered life and a very important function within the contemporary framework of life. Wherever girls have turned to some vital form of the apostolate, the marks of frustration, neurosis, loneliness and unhappiness have indeed begun to disappear. Life is not really as difficult as it seems. God's way is easy and includes everyone.

The Tragedy of Superficial Union

The tragedy of the married woman today can be traced to a misunderstanding about the nature of human love. We are made, says the Church, in the image and likeness of God. The modern world contradicts this: We are made, it says, in the image and likeness of animals. The union of a man and woman in marriage, says the Church, is analogous to the union of Christ and His Church and can only be understood in that light. It is a spiritual union, expressed through the union of bodies. The union of man and woman in marriage, says the world, is like the mating of animals, to which is attached a little more delicacy and cerebration because we are higher animals.

So the world prepares young people for marriage by teaching them physiology and the techniques of making love, and sends them into marriage (armed with contraceptive devices) physically mature but spiritually infantile.

As the marriage relationship becomes (as it must) progressively more intolerable, the publishers belch forth a mountain of books giving further instructions on the art of eroticism, and finally society shepherds the aggrieved partners singly onto the psychologist's couch, and on to the divorce court.

There virtually is no such thing as sexual incompatibility. The root trouble is the lack of spiritual harmony, and behind that a deficient spiritual development or a complete absence of spiritual orientation. How could marriage possibly succeed?

But let us return to the married woman. She has to love someone wholly. *Whom* does she love? She ought, of course, to love God and her husband as Christ's intermediary but most times she does not.

There is a natural tendency for women to love their husbands as though their husbands were God, were indeed the woman's final end. This is owing to woman's great need to love and give herself wholly, and it always leads to disaster. If the husband becomes her god the wife becomes subordinate to him in a disastrous way. She takes her standards from him (what is good is what pleases him, what is bad he doesn't like), whereas she is supposed to be the member of the family who preserves the moral standards which come from God. Her entire happiness hinges on him, and he is often a poor enough specimen. She becomes jealous, she demands much more of him in time and attention than he wants to give. Eventually the husband will be unable to tolerate this unnatural worship, accompanied as it usually is by frequent tears and emotional outbursts, and the woman will be driven to a nervous breakdown. Or else she will discover in one shattering blow that her god is a clay idol and be so disillusioned she will hate him.

If a woman doesn't love God supremely, and chances not to worship her husband, there is always the possibility of gross over-attachment to her children. Under the guise of maternal solicitude a vast multitude of woman are seeking a self-satisfaction in their children, making their sons overdependent on them and robbing their daughters of real lives of their own. Enough evidence of this sort of thing is at every hand to omit any elaboration here.

Or the married woman, like the single woman, can love herself. All loves reduce in the end to self-love or love of God, but those who love another during their lifetime have not yet settled in self-love even if they haven't attained God. Determined, premeditated self-love, as in the newly-married girl who loves clothes inordinately and wants no children, is like premature self-damnation. It's like making the final choice between God and self on the very threshold of life.

THE NEW PAGANISM

Paganism has always been marked by the degradation of women. Whether in cultured Athens or Hindu India or ancient or modern China, you will look in vain for the regard for women with which Christianity marked Western society. The degradation takes two forms: women are reduced to slave-like work and to objects of pleasure. We are returning to paganism with ever more swift strides in our society, and again it is marked by the two signs of women's degradation.

The emancipation movement has ended in women's slavery. The myriads of office and factory girls, regimented, depersonalized, with their every gesture prescribed and tabulated, are the armies of slaves on whom the new paganism is being built. Superficially it does not seem so because, for the moment at least, we encourage our new slaves to dress like Hollywood stars and we appease their appetite for life by the vicarious excitement of the movies, radio and pulp stories. We even pay them well, but it is a quarter of a century since Belloc reminded us that slavery is still slavery even if it is well paid–and cushioned about with television sets and double chocolate sundaes.

The moral debacle, plus divorce, birth control and other "enlightened" measures, has resulted in the reduction of women to a pseudo-prostitution, of which the wolf call (which so many poor ignorant women think flattering) is the symbol.

It is into this atmosphere, this post-Christian situation, that the young girl of today emerges from adolescence. For her it will be like starting all over again to work for the true emancipation which Christ came to bring her. She can no longer drain out the last dregs of happiness and dignity left by a residual Christianity, but has to forge a new path in the manner of Sts. Agatha and Agnes. But not quite in their way because they were lone Christian martyrs, defying worldly parents and a pagan society. The modern Catholic girl has the opportunity of uniting with a multitude of others in the lay apostolate, not so much to defy an inevitable authority and suffer death as (through the lay apostolate) to take advantage of what freedom of action is left to bring Christ, purity and happiness to a dispossessed younger generation whose elders have not seen fit to pass on their residual Christianity. But like the early martyrs, the young women of today may well be repudiated and cast out by their materialistic parents.

Not Less Love, but More

There is only one answer to the tragedy of the women who are making modern society quite literally a vale of tears, and that is an ordering and an increase in their love. It is pathetic to see the pseudo-solutions which the popular magazines hold out to women whose problems they often see quite clearly, and whose unhappiness has certainly not escaped them (as has not the potentialities of exploiting them for profit). How can they give any but superficial remedies? How can they suggest anything except what might deaden the pain (sometimes at the expense of virtue)? Bridge is no remedy. Helena Rubinstein does not hold the key to happiness. A new dress won't do it. Neither will an affair, a raise, a cruise or a good book.

Unlike the indifferent husband, Christ welcomes love and total devotion, and reciprocates a thousandfold. Unlike children, Christ does not outgrow His desire for our affection. Unlike the world, Christ forgives us, no matter how far we have fallen. He can purify the impure, as He perfected the woman taken in adultery.

The central fact of the case is that women need to love tremendously, and there is only one Person whom they can safely and satisfactorily love: Christ. And the more disordered their present loves, the more whole-hearted will have to be their conversion to a love of Christ.

There is no remedy for modern woman's tragedy except Christ, and wherever Christ is introduced all human relationships begin immediately to straighten themselves out.

THE LATTER DAY

Elaine Malley

A grandmother from New York, with her own nest two-thirds empty, discusses the "empty nest" period in a woman's life.

Middle age is a spectre which looms on every woman's horizon more or less vaguely and distantly. Today more than ever, with the modern accent on youth, it is screened out of our consciousness as much as possible by an infinity of curious distractions and illusions. Even when it is actually upon us, many of us tend to ignore its presence, aping youthful mannerisms and activities, and grasping frantically at any scientific discovery, from hair dyes to hormones, that promises to prolong the effect of juvenescence. At the heart of all this make-believe, which is harmless enough in itself, lies a horrible reality. We are not only worshippers of youth, we are, as a nation, stricken by a sort of spiritual infantilism. It is no wonder that age is no longer respected. Robbed of its supernatural vigor, it has the effect of arrested growth—of deformity. Maturity and adulthood, and, in time, senility, take possession of our bodies, but everything in our civilization contributes toward the perpetuation of the state of atrophy in which we keep our souls.

One of the charming features of C. S. Lewis's *Perelandra* was the Green Lady's use of the word "older." She made it synonymous with "wiser." Of course, she lived in a veiled planet that had not been subjected to the stultifying breath of malice. Time and progress were consonant there. Experience was accompanied by enhanced dignity, for it did not have the implication it has here of contact and enlarged acquaintance with evil, so that the "wiser" man always comes out "sadder."

That we despise and fear age is an indication of how far we have fallen below a purely human standard of values; for even in pagan cultures age held a place of honor for its guardianship of traditions which had been verified and transformed by personal experience into rich stores of wisdom. But Christianity has bestowed upon age a much higher distinction, and it is because we are the heirs of a Christian heritage that the highest human values are not good enough for us. Sustained and nourished by a continuity of grace, the Christian soul should increase in holiness as it advances in years. The irrational and negative innocence of children which we prize and admire so much today is small and frangible in comparison to the towering and triumphant innocence of a soul whose will to love and serve, sinking ever deeper roots in Christ, has withstood through the years the storms and buffetings of the world and the flesh and the Devil. It is even over-shadowed in God's eyes by the dazzling radiance of the soul of the repentant sinner, whose scarlet, through the compassionate mercy of our Savior, has become whiter than snow.

STAGES ON THE ROAD

The achievement of an adult, positive, willful goodness is the secret of growing old gracefully. It is not, however, to be won without effort. Every stage in life has its own attendant difficulties and challenges, which make or mar us. Those of middle age are likely to be more subtle, more oblique in approach because they are not marked by any definite physical or social milestone, as other stages are. There is the child's first day in school, the first physical manifestation of puberty, the day of graduation, the wedding day, the day the first baby is born, and so on. But there is no perceptible first grey hair or first day of elderliness. Most of us have been middle-aged for some time before we realize it. For the mother of the family this is a crucial season, calling generally for a complete reorientation of her habits of life. Sometimes a woman who up to this point faced tremendous trials and difficulties with remarkable courage and gallantry becomes suddenly a whiner, querulous and fault-finding. Frequently it seems that the lazy, selfish woman makes a more successful adjustment at this time than the one who has always put her family first. But this is only a surface judgment, for the self-centered woman, never having acquired the habit of sacrifice, has little or no adjustment to make. So easily, however, can a person's noblest virtues be put to the service of ignoble motives, it is possible that this habit of sacrifice, which developed so spontaneously in compliance with growing responsibilities, may have hardened into an instrument for making herself indispensable. To be truly effective the habit of sacrifice must never be separated from a habit which keeps the soul supple and resilient.

The most important thing a woman can do at this time is face the fact that she is being called to a new status in her vocation. She should make a survey of her terrain and get her new bearings. As long as she clings to an "as you were" mentality, as long as she clings to the past, she will have no hands free to accept the torrents of grace that her new state in life exposes her to. Some of the circumstances to which she must adjust are: a change in her relationship with her children, an intensification of her relationship with her husband, and an alteration in her own personal duties and responsibilities.

THE YOUNG SHOOTS

It is difficult for a woman to accept the fact that her children are now adults. Sometimes this is due to reluctance to relinquish an authority which has become a source of personal satisfaction. Sometimes it is due to fear that the youngsters will make irrevocable mistakes. Let her remember that when they were first learning to walk she had to steel herself against rushing to their comfort at every bump and fall. So now, too, she must stand by and let them make their own errors. There was a time for teaching and warning and preparing. That time is past. Experience is something that cannot be transferred.   Unsolicited advice falls on impatient and inattentive ears. The young people are too engrossed in learning what life itself has to teach them to pay heed to any more words. They want to make their own decisions and undergo their own trials.

On the whole, most mothers are generally content with the careers chosen by their offspring, as long as they follow a familiar, time-honored pattern. Marriage brings the expectation of grand-children, sweet in themselves, priceless in the rich portent of new generations bearing the fruit of her marriage on to a sort of temporal immortality. Priesthood and the religious life are generally welcome, too, with a certain awed humility and a sense of gaining an ambassador in heaven to represent the family. But there are two courses which do cause dissension and unhappiness between parents and their adult children.

THE APOSTATE

One of them is that of the *apostate*. Far from depreciating the discord caused by his dissension, it should be regarded as an indication of moral health. Parents are within their rights in condemning bad marriages, drunkenness, shady professions and other manifestations of ungodly living. Much of the present-day prevalence of loose morals comes from an idolatry of one's flesh and blood that embraces the sin with the sinner; an abject pusillanimity that pretends to ignore the presence of evil rather than risk open encounter with it; and a human respect that will go to any lengths to avoid being labelled "intolerance."

More painful to the mother than outward recognition and censure of her child's guilt is the inward knowledge of it, its acknowledgment before God. She haunts His judgment seat, pleading for mercy, and after having explained how completely she is to blame, she racks her memory and ransacks her conscience for any additional scrap over which she may plead *mea culpa* and so find further extenuation for the guilt of the sinner. Every sacrifice, every mortification, every prayer which she can make or induce others to make, goes for his special intention.

Her concern is moving, but it should be tempered with realism. It is possible for her to lose her psychological balance in thus obliterating the limits of personal responsibility. God knows the extenuating circumstances, He is merciful, and He "wills not the death of a sinner, but that he repent and be converted." She cannot help suffering for her wayward child, but she must never allow this sorrow to disturb an inner serenity where hope burns like a vigil lamp, trusting in God's infinite power to bring good out of evil.

THE LAY APOSTLE

Another cause of family contention these days is the *lay apostolate*. In certain cases the youngsters themselves may be responsible for the disfavor with which the movement is regarded.

Having seen the truth in a new light, they think they are seeing it for the first time, and they rush home, fired with enthusiasm, to preach it to their parents. Much of what they have to say is an echo of what the parents have tried in vain for years to instill into them (such as the necessity for work!). This may be merely amusing or only mildly exasperating in itself. But it is sometimes accompanied by an attitude of levity toward traditions and customs the parents have always held dear, or by unnecessary criticism of the parents. These breaches of filial charity may represent only an initial reflex, to disappear with the deepening of the spiritual life, but they may also be sufficient to create a prejudice against the apostolate.

In other cases, however, the resentment is more deeply rooted, and no amount of prudence and diplomacy on the part of the young apostles seems to be able to allay the fear and suspicion with which the apostolate is regarded. It is so new and daring. Its very nature is incompatible with an undue affection for tepidity, for conformity, for sterile inoffensiveness. It shoots like a bolt of lightning straight to the heart of the sickness of our time, a sickness which a self-righteous civilization has tried to ignore or disguise by burying it under layers of silence and pseudo-respectability. The mother must pass from revulsion at the exposure of its wounds, through disbelief that the sickness is curable, to the realization that even here Christ's healing mercy can penetrate, and that one of His instruments for our time is the lay apostolate. It is a long way for her to go, but at its end lies a new vision, a richer realization of the truths of our faith, and an incredulous gratitude that God should have chosen the son or daughter of His handmaid for His service in such a special way.

The man of the house

Children are the strongest unifying factor in marriage, but there is a sense in which it is inevitable that they should come between husband and wife. Just as a woman when she is married must "think the things of the world, how she may please her husband," so a wife, when she has children, must think the things of the nursery, how she may raise her children. In many homes the man has a pretty sorry time of it as soon as the children begin to make their appearance. He who should be the first to be considered is often the last, if he gets any consideration at all.

Our national women's magazines have been insisting for some years that a woman should keep up with her husband *intellectually*—which generally means being able to discuss with him the daily newspaper, an occasional best seller, and perhaps some technical pursuit or hobby. Perhaps there was a time when a woman had to struggle to keep abreast of the cultural status of her husband. But it seems that today the position is reversed. Many men, geared to the industrial machine, have had to strip from their lives nearly everything not concerned with the business of making a living. They have had little or no time for the development of a taste for the finer things of life. This has resulted in a process of deterioration which has been very clearly expressed by John Stuart-Mill: "Capacity for the nobler feeling is in most natures a very tender plant....Men lose their high aspirations as they lose their intellectual tastes, because they have not time or opportunity for indulging them; and they addict themselves to inferior pleasures, not because they deliberately prefer them, but because they are either the only ones to which they have access, or the only ones which they are any longer capable of enjoying."

Many women, on the other hand, freed by home appliances from the heaviest drudgery that housekeeping used to entail, have been able to lead a more well-rounded existence. The necessity for caring for the children has brought out in them unsuspected talents and kept their human sensitivities from drying up. Through the children some have come into contact with the local community and its problems, and have taken part in wholesome social activities. Some have used their leisure for a great deal of cultural flapdoodle, in the spirit of delivering a deliberate slap-in-the-face at their long-suffering mates. But some have spent it in prayer and good works, with the results that it is the women who are the leaders in matters pertaining to religion, it is the women who *make* their husbands comply with their religious obligations.

This is a dangerous state of affairs for both of them. The man, to be happy, must be the leader; the woman, to be happy, must be led. Furthermore, a female-dominated culture is an effeminate culture, weak, erratic, inclined to hysteria. It is up to the woman to awaken her man to participation in a fuller life. Here is a situation to which she must bring the gentleness of the dove, the cunning of the serpent, and all the tenderness of her womanhood. She must realize that she has been granted special favors, while her husband, goaded by pressures from within and without the home, has been forced to overstress his role as provider, and in so doing has sacrificed some of his privileges of friend, companion, spouse, father, *person*. Now is a good time for both husband and wife to make up to each other for the years of service they have given each other through the children and for the years of involuntary neglect of each other caused by giving these things their first thought.

If separate cares and obligations have not come between the man and woman, if the years have only succeeded in bringing them closer together, then, indeed, this should be their happiest time. This is the harvest of their lives. They may contemplate their grown children together and rejoice in a sense of accomplishment. They may rejoice in each other, too, in a way which was never possible before, for they have learned wisdom with the years, and no longer expect perfection from each other—only the comfort of a deep and rich familiarity, the time-tested happiness of knowing all the ins and outs of the loved one's personality, and basking in his love and devotion.

THE NEW STATUS

An important step in the ascent to a new status is the disengagement of the affections from the things of the past. In this direction an appeal is made to the inner conscious-ness for sacrifice at every stage of life. Sometimes the appeal becomes a peremptory demand, and a vital faculty, or a dearly loved one, is snatched away. When such a trial comes the acquiescent soul may take comfort in the knowledge that God Himself is taking a hand in stripping the soul of impediments and drawing it closer to Himself.

One particularly difficult cross that comes with increas-ing age is that of declining health and strength. A woman who has always taken care of those about her may suddenly find herself helpless and utterly dependent on the charity of those whom she once served as a matter of course. This is perhaps the most dreaded of prospects—the thing from which most women beg in their prayers to be spared. And yet it is a very special vocation, a call to become a victim soul and to share in the sufferings of Our Lord's Passion. So much suffering in the world is wasted! Here is an op-portunity to make up for it by making an interior act of surrender and by offering up, not only the physical pain, but the more excruciating distress caused by voluntary or involuntary slights or indignities.

In fact, everything that comes with later life can be made the instrument of an individual apostolate. If I were asked to choose one word which best expresses the duty of a woman at this time, the thing that she can really give her time to with profit, it would be the word *rejoice.* This is the time of the rendering of talents, the crowning point of her earthly vocation. It can be a foretaste of heaven. There will be some trepidation and anxiety mixed with her rejoicing: she has not done as well as she could, she has made many mistakes. And as long as she lives she will never be wholly free from concern about those God has given her to love. But she should never let that concern degenerate into ineffectual worry. It is her spur to prayer, to real prayer and meditation, the keynote of which will be inexpressible gratitude, joy in His gifts. The hand-pieced quilts our grandmothers made, the innumerable knit goods—what were they but something for the fingers to be occupied with, a secular rosary—while the mind dwelt on God's goodness and contemplated His blessings?